Praise for *The Affluent Entrepreneur*

"Patrick Snow does it again! The speaker and coach who brought us *Creating Your Own Destiny* picks up right where he left off, with *The Affluent Entrepreneur*. His message is timeless while the timing is perfect. This book needs to be in the hands of everyone who is interested in making a life, not just making a living. The principles in this book are sound, timely, rich, and inspirational. Bottom line, a great read and one I'm grateful to have on my bookshelf to reference for a lifetime."

—**Randall Broad, Coauthor of**
It's An Extraordinary Life—Don't Miss It
www.ItsAnExtraordinaryLife.com

"After the 2007 economic downturn, it's apparent the old ways of building financial security are unreliable and outdated. In *The Affluent Entrepreneur*, Patrick Snow offers 20 powerful prosperity principles that, when followed, will give you income security to withstand any economic climate and provide peace of mind and the time and freedom to enjoy your dream life. Patrick shares stories of his own and other entrepreneurs' real-life trials and triumphs, stories that will inspire you to take back control of your life from an employer and put it in your hands where it belongs."

—**Flora Morris Brown, PhD,**
Author of *Color Your Life Happy*
www.ColorYourLifeHappy.com

"This book shows you how to overcome the biggest single challenge to succeeding as an entrepreneur. It is powerful, practical, and immediately useful. Read it cover to cover."

—**Albert Mensah, Author of**
OK Means Opportunity Knocking
www.AlbertMensah.com

"These 20 principles are essential to building a solid foundation for your success. Applying this book to your life will accelerate your journey to success."

—**Britt Santowski, Author of**
The Three Strategies of the Unstoppable Woman
www.TheThreeStrategies.com

"Every now and then a book comes along that provides the right perspective at the right time. *The Affluent Entrepreneur* is one of those books. You can't reach a new level if you can't define it. Patrick has done an amazing job at helping entrepreneurs to do both."

—**Kevin Hocker, Author of** *The Success Compass*
www.TheSuccessCompass.com

"Patrick Snow is dead on! If you want a better understanding of the ins and outs of being influential in business, you have got to read this book!"

—**Dr. LaVerne Adams, Author of** *Driven by Destiny*
www.DivineDestinyDoctor.com

"Are you in fear of being laid off? Or, have you been terminated already? Read this book and learn how you never have to work for someone else again. You can create your own successful business and achieve financial independence on your own terms. Patrick Snow will show you how."

—**Terri Dunevant, Award-Winning**
Author of *The Staircase Principle*
www.WinCourage.com

"This book is both eye-opening and inspiring; it provides a well-defined path to obtaining an abundant life filled with joy, peace, and the excitement of tomorrow! I know this to be true because I know Patrick Snow!"

—**Frank Reed, Author of** *In God*
We Trust: Dollars & Sense!
www.BottomLineMinistries.org

"Patrick's message is life-changing! He not only cares about people, but also is generous, genuine, loving, and WALKS his talk. If you want to live your dream, do what he does. Read this book and you will learn how to achieve prosperity."

—**Laurie Hardie, Author of** *Reviving the Dream*
www.RevivingTheDream.com

"Taking full responsibility for one's own financial health (becoming an entrepreneur) can be a scary thing, but it can open the doors to a life of unlimited prosperity, security, and fulfillment. Patrick Snow inspires and shows you how to take that daring leap!"

—**Dr. Marvin Kunikiyo, Author of**
Revolutionizing Your Health
www.RevolutionizingYourHealth.com

"Patrick has nailed it with this book. The timing of his wisdom and the knowledge contained in these pages is an excellent guide for those seeking to create their own financial destiny! In a time of great economic change, get this book now and follow the sage advice and wisdom it contains!"

—**Tony Rubleski, Best-selling**
Author of *Mind Capture*
www.MindCaptureGroup.com

"Patrick Snow is one of those rare individuals who is the real deal. He is brilliant when it comes to doing what it takes to make dreams happen for his clients and readers. His passion shows through in everything he does and no one feels it more than his readers. Read every page of this book and you will learn how to become an 'Affluent Entrepreneur.' Do yourself a favor and read Patrick's books, get his coaching, and apply his message to your life so you can soar."

—**Denny Andrews, Author of**
Confessions of a Mortgage Insider
www.DennyAndrewsConsulting.com

"If you have ever met Patrick in person or heard him speak, you would know that he is an entrepreneur dedicated to helping you succeed while being both passionate and inspiring. The fact that this comes through in his writing is amazing! I highly recommend you read both *Creating Your Own Destiny* and *The Affluent Entrepreneur* if you want to live your best life now."

—**Jeffery Bow, Author of**
Stop Thinking, Start Believing
www.JeffBowCoaching.com

"Patrick Snow has done it again by producing yet another great life and business tool with his new book, *The Affluent Entrepreneur*. Patrick offers you a proven method of success that will help you achieve prosperity in every area of your life. Patrick's entrepreneurship blueprint has helped me soar to the top in my business, family, and personal life. This book will EMPOWER you to do the same and thrive beyond measure!"

—**Malika L. Anderson, Author of**
The Real Woman's Guide To
An Almost-Perfect Life
www.MalikaAnderson.com

"Patrick Snow shows how to put your life and finances in your own control. This is not one of those get-rich-quick books with flawed financial strategies. Rather, this is an inspiring, yet practical, book about how to achieve emotional peace of mind and complete freedom through building your own business. Patrick Snow shows you how to break free of your doubts and insecurities to become an Affluent Entrepreneur!"

—**Brett Clay, Author of** *Selling Change*
www.SellingChange.com

"*The Affluent Entrepreneur* will motivate you to master time-tested techniques to better your business and your life. Master teacher Patrick Snow will show you not only what to do but HOW to do it!"

—**Kristopher L. Walton, MSW,**
Author of *Navigating Your Mind*
www.NavigatingYourMind.com

"Patrick walks his talk! He's an entrepreneur par excellence. He knows what to do and how to do it. So, if you want to be successful, and be an Affluent Entrepreneur, this book is a 'must' read!"

—**Susan Friedmann, CSP,**
Author of *Riches in Niches*
www.RichesInNiches.com

"Patrick's first book, *Creating Your Own Destiny*, has stood the test of time. Now with *The Affluent Entrepreneur*, I have another influential tool to help guide me to even greater financial success. I have rarely met another person who has steered my life in the right direction as Patrick has."

—**Shannon S. Carlson,**
Author of *Living Your Life in Balance*
www.LivingYourLifeInBalance.com

"If you are serious about living life on your own terms, then you must read and apply the principles in this powerful book to your business!"

—**Dr. Taylor Clark,**
Author of *Beating All Odds*
www.BeatingAllOdds.com

THE AFFLUENT ENTREPRENEUR

THE AFFLUENT ENTREPRENEUR

20 Proven Principles for Achieving Prosperity

PATRICK SNOW

WILEY

John Wiley & Sons, Inc.

ISBN 978-0-470-60158-7 (cloth)
ISBN 978-0-470-92309-2 (ebk)
ISBN 978-0-470-92310-8 (ebk)
ISBN 978-0-470-92311-5 (ebk)

Printed in the United States of America

10 9 8 7 6 5 4 3 2 1

To my two sons, Samuel and Jacob.

You are the reason I work on my passions.
My two books are written for you both.
I hope that long after my time on earth
has passed, you and your children will benefit
from this message of entrepreneurship.
I love you both, and I am so proud to be your father!

To my mother and father, Jack and Lois Snow.

You are the best parents a child could have.
I became the person I am today because
of your love and belief in me.
Thank you for encouraging me to make
my own money as a kid (mowing yards,
shoveling snow, and having a paper route).
I love you both and am eternally grateful for all your support!

To you, the reader.

It is my honor and privilege to assist you on your
journey to becoming an Affluent Entrepreneur!
May you find peace and enjoy prosperity in life.

SOAR

CREATING
YOUR OWN
DESTINY

EXECUTE

DREAM

PLAN

CONTENTS

ACKNOWLEDGMENTS

I would like to thank all of you who have made an impact on my life. There are too many to list here so I will just name a few. I will forever be grateful for your support and belief in my vision.

Denny Andrews, David Angelo, Soumangue Basse, Dave Beauchamp, Randy Broad, Les Brown, Bryan Caplovitz, Bettina Carey, Taylor Clark, Mark Colyer, Ian Cordell, Matt DiMaio, James Donaldson, Brent Duskin, Bob Erdmann, Lauren Freestone, Susan Friedmann, Rick Frommer, Tom Glazier, Thom Hamilton, Cedric Harris, Burke Hedges, Michael Helgeson, Ray Higdon, Matthew Holt, Howard Howell, Nancy Jacques, Dan Janal, Jerry Jenkins, Nancy Juetten, Paul Kadillak, Christopher Kent, Jake Kevorkian, Peter Knox, Eric Lofholm, Jeannine Mallory, Og Mandino, Jennifer Manlowe, Bill McCarrick, John McLelland, Albert Mensah, Mike Mezack, Christopher Paraldi, Kate Phillips, Tim Polk, Dan Poynter, Shiloh Schroeder, Elana Schulman, Tyler Tichelaar, Brian Tracy, Shannon Vargo, Rob Van Pelt, Tony Wall, Mary West, David Wood, and Zig Ziglar.

Building Income Security

> The best time to plant a tree is 20 years ago;
> the second-best time is today.
> —Chinese Proverb

Whether you realize it or not, you only have three financial options to consider throughout your life when it comes to determining your income-earning ability. The option you choose will ultimately determine your destiny. Your choice will not only decide your financial and emotional peace of mind, but it also will determine whether or not you will achieve what the subtitle of this book promises: *Prosperity*.

Option One is to become an employee and create wealth for someone else. Option Two is to become an unsuccessful business owner and struggle financially. Option Three is to become an *Affluent Entrepreneur* and soar in life. With these options in mind, this book was written to help you successfully select Option Three so that you can indeed create your own destiny and experience prosperity in all areas of your life.

Before we begin, it is important that I ask you some questions to help you make the right selection. Do you have anxiety when it comes to your finances? Are you tired of having someone else looking over your shoulder telling you how and when you need to work? Are you tired of working overtime and having to beg for vacation time or to request time off to be there for a family member? Is your boss an *idiot*? Are you worried about layoffs? Do you feel trapped at your job? Are you tired of running a business and always wondering why you never have enough paying customers to meet your basic operating expenses, let alone turn a profit? Have you come to the same conclusion I have that it is virtually impossible to achieve wealth as an employee? If you answered "Yes" to any or all of these questions, then the financial answers you seek can be found in reading this book.

Let's face it—sooner or later, we all realize that having a good secure job is NOT the answer. In today's environment, such a job has become extinct just like the dinosaurs. Because job security *no longer* exists, our challenge is to create income security, and that is exactly what the Affluent Entrepreneur is a master at—creating multiple streams of income, without additional effort, that will pay him or her residually for life, thereby allowing the Affluent Entrepreneur to make a life instead of settling for less and making a living.

In recent times, the world has changed, especially beginning in 2007 with the real estate and mortgage meltdown. As a result, workers are now faced with new, never before experienced challenges. It must top the list (so far) of the anxiety-provoking, ulcer-producing questions of the twenty-first century: *What can I do to survive this grueling economy and stave off financial devastation?* You might be surprised at the number of people who fret over this question every day. You are *not* alone! Yet, so few search for the answer—and it's out there! In my first book, *Creating Your Own Destiny*, I showed how you can predetermine your future by becoming an independent business owner and leveraging the free-enterprise system. In *The Affluent Entrepreneur*, my goal is to help you (and other soon-to-be or existing business owners) to win in the game of free enterprise and thrive financially during both times of economic uncertainty and abundance.

The economy and investment strategies, as we once knew them to be, will never be the same. Financial tactics and practices once viewed as uncommon or desperate moves have now become part of the norm. These include foreclosures, loan modifications, government bailouts, downsizing, layoffs, and personal or business bankruptcies. Businesses that had been a part of the financial fabric of our society for generations, such as Lehman Brothers, Merrill

Lynch, and Washington Mutual, have either been purchased by other financial powerhouses, or they've been wiped off the map and are now gone forever.

This unpredictable financial environment can—and will—devastate your finances if you rely on *yesterday's* outdated methods to provide for your family *today*. If you have a *job*, then your financial security depends on your employer's success—something you often cannot control. On the other hand, if you own a business, then you can depend on yourself, your creativity, and your willingness to work hard—things you *can* control—to determine how prosperous and successful you want to be. I'm convinced, *now* more than ever, that the best way to create your own destiny and achieve financial security is through owning and operating your own business!

As more people are laid off and now must cope with the reality of being unable to provide for their families, many have discovered there's a better way. They're becoming business owners, and you can do the same. And best of all—it's work they love. They're creating their own destinies, and they're on the way to realizing the American Dream (regardless of what country they live in). Many of these new business owners are challenged because they've received little or no training in how to succeed in business. Also, many long-time business owners continue to struggle and need guidance to take their businesses to the next level and beyond. The 20 principles in *The Affluent Entrepreneur* will provide you with a blueprint to help you take charge of your financial future whether or not you are a business owner yet. You will learn how to thrive during a time when your employee counterparts exist in a world of panic, frustration, and anxiety, just hoping to keep their jobs. This book will show you how to learn to fish for yourself rather than being handed a fish on payday.

As we get started, let me define a few terms that will help you better understand this book's title. My definition of Affluent Entrepreneurs (AEs) are *risk takers who have achieved financial and emotional peace of mind and now enjoy complete freedom in all areas of life as a direct result of success in building their own business.* The Affluent Entrepreneur works out of choice—not out of need. The Affluent Entrepreneur has a sizeable amount of money set aside for emergencies. Affluent Entrepreneurs love what they do. Affluent Entrepreneurs pay cash for virtually everything and never use other people's money (OPM) except for business strategy purposes. Affluent Entrepreneurs are dedicated to giving both time and money to help others in need. Most important, an Affluent Entrepreneur keeps family as a top priority. My number one primary goal in writing this book is to show *you* and your loved ones, how you too can become an Affluent Entrepreneur!

Now that you know the definition for the title of this book, let's define a few other key words in the title and subtitle. *Webster's Dictionary* defines an "entrepreneur" as *one who starts a business or another venture that promises economic gain but also entails risks.* Another definition is *a risk-taker who has the skills and initiative to establish a business.* No need to worry here; if you don't feel you currently have these skills, the principles in this book are designed to provide you with the knowledge and confidence needed to become a successful business owner.

The word "affluent" is an adjective defined as *having an abundance of wealth, property, or other material goods; prosperous; rich. Abounding in anything, abundant, flowing freely, an affluent fountain.* Finally "prosperity" is a noun defined as *a successful, flourishing, or thriving condition especially in financial respects; good fortune.* Combine these three words together (affluent + entrepreneur + prosperity), and you have a very powerful formula and career compass to guide you in solving many of the career and financial challenges you may currently be facing.

Many extreme liberals, other politicians, and biblical theologians have argued or suggested that pursuing wealth is in some way bad or immoral. Some have argued that the word "affluent" is actually a bad word that assumes rich people have in some way achieved their wealth unethically or immorally. Some of these folks believe that all who have achieved prosperity are in some way bad or will be judged by our Creator in a negative way. For those who make this argument, I encourage them to read John 10:10. This Bible verse is considered by many to be the dividing line between what Christians believe about affluence:

> The thief comes only in order to steal and kill and destroy. I came that they may have and enjoy life, and have it in abundance (to the full, till it overflows).

This verse may be one of the least understood and most misinterpreted verses in the Bible. My belief is that God does indeed want his people to achieve abundance so that they can give back *more* to those in need. A perfect example of how affluence can benefit the masses is evident in work that Bill Gates, one of the wealthiest and most affluent people of all time, does with the Bill and Melinda Gates Foundation, which gives hundreds of millions of dollars in health aid and computers to people all over the world to improve their lives.

Now that you know where I stand on this financial debate, I want you to keep one thing in mind. This book is *not* a road map on how to accumulate material possessions! Rather, this book is a road map to help you take total control of your life so that you can have complete freedom to pursue your passions and to be present for your family, your friends, your community, and others who may be in need. By the end of this book, you will come to comprehend that this book is *not* about accumulating and receiving, but rather it is about giving, helping, and educating those in need so they will become able to support themselves and enjoy life the way it was intended to be enjoyed.

Where would we be today if it were not for people with creative vision who decided to take the risk of becoming entre-preneurs to bring their dreams to fruition? We all know how people like Thomas Edison and Henry Ford took risks to make their visions become reality; their entrepreneurial spirits revolu-tionized how people live, and we are all still reaping the benefits of their visions today. You may say, "Yes, but that was over a hundred years ago. What Ford and Edison did can't be done in today's economic climate." I beg to differ.

In each chapter of this book, I will include an "Affluent Entrepreneur Profile" to highlight altogether 20 great entrepreneurs from the last 200 years, some from the distant past like Andrew Carnegie and John D. Rockefeller, and others from recent years such as Bill Gates of Microsoft, and Larry Page and Sergey Brin, cofounders of Google. Each of these Affluent Entrepreneurs had the vision and made the effort, often despite incredible odds, to become successful and to live an affluent life.

The Affluent Entrepreneurs showcased here are in no particular order. They are not ranked 1–20 based on total net worth. They are men and woman, black and white, living and dead, young and old. I researched a large number of entrepreneurs and selected the finest examples from a variety of industries—steel to automobiles, entertainment to fashion and the Internet—to provide you with different perspectives. Additionally, my selection criteria were also based on the principle I believed each one best fit. Several of them arguably could fit under numerous categories because they utilized several of the principles in this book to achieve their wealth. Also note that not all of them are billionaires, several of them are "just millionaires." What a problem to have—to be "just a millionaire!"

Nowhere in this book am I promising that you will become a millionaire or billionaire. However, my guarantee to you is that if you apply the principles laid out in this book, you will experience explosive growth in your business and become an Affluent Entrepreneur as a result.

I've included profiles of Affluent Entrepreneurs in hopes that not only will you learn 20 proven principles to achieving prosperity, but you will also learn 20 character traits of Affluent Entrepreneurs. Count how many of these traits match your personality. At the end of the book, I'll provide a little quiz on those character traits so that you can assess your likelihood of becoming an Affluent Entrepreneur. I'll also provide you with the Affluent Entrepreneur

Creed so you'll have a constant reminder of the principles by which you should live and do business.

Finally, please note that the Affluent Entrepreneurs whose stories I tell are held up only as examples of how to succeed in business. While many of them were not perfect in their family or personal lives, each one selected has possessed a majority of the Affluent Entrepreneur traits. I am aware that some of these Affluent Entrepreneurs are far from being saints, and I am not asking you to aspire to being like them. I am simply suggesting that if you emulate their business strategies, you have a better chance of becoming successful. In fact, you can also learn from their relationship and family mistakes so you can avoid making the same errors in judgment. While being an Affluent Entrepreneur is highly important to me, my faith and family come first, and I encourage you to follow that same principle. I'll talk more about such priorities throughout the book. Ultimately, I hope the stories of these Affluent Entrepreneurs, and my own stories, will inspire you to believe just how possible it is for you to become an Affluent Entrepreneur yourself.

Over the years, numerous people have written books about financial freedom, free enterprise, and wealth creation. The market is flooded with fantastic books proclaiming various investment strategies and real estate models as a way to achieve great wealth. I'm going to go out on a limb here and say that some of these concepts are now slightly flawed because they are out of date with today's economic market. The financial rules followed in pre-2007, which produced huge profits for investors, may no longer be the sure bet they once were. Often, it is difficult to know whether you are investing during a rising curve or falling curve. When the housing bubble burst in mid-2007, we learned that putting money in real estate and investing the old-school way weren't the safe bets they once were. These two strategies no longer guarantee financial security.

Because of these changes in the financial marketplace, you'll find that *The Affluent Entrepreneur* isn't the same as traditional books in the personal growth and self-help genre. Rather, it is a *business* book designed to provide real-life business solutions to your financial challenges. This book isn't about investing in the stock market, real estate, or building a large retirement income. Many other fantastic books in the marketplace can provide these investment strategies for you. Rather, this book is about soul searching to identify your innermost marketable passion and then turning that passion into a business you can own and operate—*regardless* of your background, education, or level of experience. Most important, *The Affluent Entrepreneur* is a book that will help you achieve huge success in your business. The book is about identifying problems in the marketplace, then creating a business model to solve those problems, and being paid handsomely as a result of your ingenuity!

Some of you may think this process sounds too good, or too easy, to be true. Well, as an entrepreneur myself, I empathize with you, I feel your pain, and I understand your doubt and fears. Perhaps after a layoff, you are not excited about starting from scratch pursuing a new business model. Perhaps you are worried about a reduction in your high credit score or even taking money from savings to invest in your business. You have every right to be worried about your financial future. I too was hit hard by layoffs twice during my career in high-tech sales as a result of the 9/11 tragedies and industry changes and again in 2002. While I've never had to file bankruptcy, I came very close to financial ruin back in 2004.

Faced with the reality of trying to make it in the post-9/11 economy, I had to sell our family home to steer away from bankruptcy and avoid foreclosure. I used the equity from the sale of our home to pay off all our debts and to continue to invest in my speaking, publishing, and coaching business. It hasn't been easy, but because I followed my dreams and I believe in my destiny, I am confident I can help you also to succeed on the path to becoming an Affluent Entrepreneur. It is not going to be easy—there will be calculated risks involved—but it is the best investment you can make. No other investment in the market today can offer you the same return on investment (ROI) as you will experience as a result of investing in yourself. This book is your solution, your resource, and your financial blueprint to use in your quest to become an Affluent Entrepreneur. The principles here will help you to take that leap of faith and to reap the financial rewards that result from your actions.

At age 36, I made a decision that never again would I risk my family's financial future on the success or failure of my employer. I knew I needed to break my dependency of working for "the man." The sooner I could do so, the better off our family would be. Up to that point I had been a part-time entrepreneur throughout my adult life, but it took me until I was 36 years old before I could walk away from my job on my own terms and dive in as a full-time entrepreneur. In this book, I will guide you through this same process and help you to decide when is the right time to leave the comforts of your day job and jump into your business full-time. As a result of taking this plunge during the post 9/11 economy, I almost lost everything. You too will make it through your future transition. This book will show you how.

Because of the lessons learned in 2001, and the actions I took pursuing the lifestyle of an Affluent Entrepreneur, the 2007 economic meltdown barely fazed our family. It was nothing more than a small speed bump in the road on our journey toward our destiny. Therefore, I want to help set you and your family up to become bulletproof and to thrive and build more wealth in any economic climate now or in the future. Following the principles in this book will allow you to soar in any financial market and become an Affluent Entrepreneur.

As someone in my early forties, I understand the challenges faced by many of you who are part of Generation X and Generation Y. Having given over 1,500 speaking engagements and listened to the members of my audiences, I also understand the challenges faced by the baby boomers. As a Gen Xer myself, I'm in tune with both groups, and I feel I can offer you 20 proven principles that will shorten your learning curve. Regardless of your age or entrepreneurial experience, this book will give you the knowledge, tools, and strategies for achieving prosperity as an entrepreneur. I also know what it takes to look risk square in the face and take that leap of faith to start your own businesses.

I wrote this book for you as an Entrepreneurial Blueprint to follow so that you can build a successful business—despite any adversities or circumstances you may be facing. This book is for people like you who aren't satisfied with their careers, aren't happy at work, and aren't willing to settle for less! If you are looking for a way to become a successful business owner, then I believe you are in the right place with the right resources in hand. I challenge you to read every page of this book and to apply all 20 principles to your business to maximize your profit potential.

This book is an easy-to-follow handbook for business owners. Its subtitle, "20 Proven Principles for Achieving Prosperity," reflects principles that are guaranteed to help you and other new business owners achieve success faster than you ever could have imagined. They are principles you don't pick up in college or business school. You see, I developed these principles the old-fashioned way, through trial and error—that's why I know they work. I pounded the pavement for almost 15 years in corporate sales, and then I applied what I learned in my sales career to my business. As a result, I built a very successful business in less than 10 years. Sure, I made many mistakes along the way—but I learned from every one of them, and I am going to encourage you to avoid the same mistakes I made so that you can reduce your success timetable.

In all, I have spent well over 20 years learning and developing these principles and applying them to my business, so I know these principles work. I've read more than 1,500 books about personal growth and development. I've studied the successes and failures of many successful, and not-so-successful, entrepreneurs throughout the world. I've also watched as family and friends have both succeeded and failed in business, and I have digested valuable lessons on both ends of the spectrum. This book contains real-life stories telling how the successful entrepreneurs succeeded and why the folks who didn't make it as business owners failed (both right and wrong, all for your benefit).

I challenge you to build income security for you and your family so you will never have to worry about finances again. This goal may seem easier said than done. However, I can assure you that when you apply the principles in this book to your life, you will achieve income security for your family. As a result, you will become a better person, a better spouse, a better parent to your children, and a better child to your parents. In other words, you will be able to clear your mind of financial headaches and focus on providing for the loved ones in your life not just with your money but, more important, with your time.

My goal is to help you achieve as much success as possible in the shortest amount of time possible. I will share my heart and soul with you as well as my own mistakes to help you reduce your learning curve. When you apply the principles in this book to your life and your business, you will ultimately become an Affluent Entrepreneur! I want to help you by becoming your accountability partner and your mastermind member. If I can do it, so can you.

Are you ready to begin? Do you have an open mind? Are you ready forever to leave your financial worries behind? If so, are you ready to embark on an exciting career transition that will change your life, your family, and your business forever?

Good. Then let's begin *right now*!

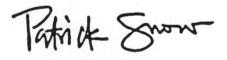

Creating Your Own Unique Product or Service

It takes as much energy to wish as it does to plan.
—Eleanor Roosevelt

In this chapter, you will learn how to identify your most marketable passions, and then turn these passions into profit to lay the foundation for becoming an Affluent Entrepreneur. You will learn how to create a unique selling proposition and how to create, develop, or acquire a product or service unlike anyone else's. You will learn how to keep your overhead low. You will learn not only how to create a business plan, but also how to implement it completely within a realistic timeframe. You will learn how to identify problems in the marketplace and how to create solutions for those problems. Finally, you will learn how Frederick Weyerhaeuser created a very unique product, and ultimately, became one of the grandest real estate investors of our time.

IDENTIFY PROBLEMS OR OPPORTUNITIES IN THE MARKETPLACE

After you've decided to become a business owner, it's important to identify your most marketable passions. Remember, you must do work that you love, so we'll go through a process of self-discovery where you'll determine your strengths and what you love to do. After answering a series of questions, I'll lead you through some steps to examine your level of success as an entrepreneur and to help you determine whether your product or service will be successful. Once you've settled on your product or service, I'll show you how to do the required market research. Then you'll learn how to write a business plan and find seed money to launch your new business.

Opportunities are all around if we open our eyes and look for them. The reason why most businesses fail is simply because they don't ask themselves the question: *Does the need for my product or service actually exist in the marketplace?* This may be the most important question a new entrepreneur can ask himself. Before throwing time and money at a business venture, the new entrepreneur must ask whether the marketplace has a true problem and whether his proposed product or service can actually solve that problem. Below are examples of Affluent Entrepreneurs who have created products or services that identified problems and then built companies to solve those problems for their customers.

My first example comes from my own region of the country in the Northwest. My family and I have lived in the Seattle area since I graduated from the University of Montana in 1991. In 1997, we moved to Bainbridge Island (located 8 miles west of Seattle across the Puget Sound, which is a 35-minute ferry ride to the city). Bainbridge Island has truly been a great place to raise our family, but there is one challenge with living there—it is very difficult to get from Bainbridge to Sea-Tac Airport for early morning flights.

Years and years ago, one of your options was to drive around the back way across two bridges to get to the airport (which is a 90-minute drive) and be stuck paying high airport parking fees. Another option was to drive your car on and off the ferry in both directions, which took less time, but you had to pay car tolls on the ferry, and you would still be stuck paying airport parking. The third option was to hope and pray that a cab was available. If there was one, you then had to hope and pray that you were not attacked by one of the cab drivers, since they would aggressively coerce you to get into their cabs if they saw you walking down the ramp with a roller bag. Finally the last option was to walk six blocks up from the ferry to catch a bus or light rail train, the problem being that these modes of transportation were six blocks straight up a hill, so not a real option when you're carrying luggage.

Several years ago, Paul (he provides such great service that everyone on Bainbridge just knows him as "Paul" although his full name is Harpal S. Baul) recognized that in Seattle, a metropolitan population of around 3.8 million people, he could start a town car/limo service that virtually and exclusively served the 20,000 people living on Bainbridge Island to help us eliminate the stresses of getting from the ferry terminal to the airport, and upon our return arrivals, serve our needs by getting us from the airport to the ferry terminal.

Paul now has 12 cars and the nicest drivers I have ever met. In fact, Paul loves his job so much that he too continues to drive and serve his customers. We residents of Bainbridge call him 24/7/365, and he always has a limo/town car waiting for us at the curb taking us to and from the airport. If you can believe it, he provides this service for a flat fee that is the same price as a cab, or sometimes a little less since cab meters continue to run when there is a lot of traffic.

One time when I was traveling, I had scheduled two speeches in one week, one speech in San Diego and the other in Minneapolis. Since I always try to limit my nights away from home, I decided to come home that Tuesday night to be with my family before flying out yet a second time in the same week on Wednesday morning. And so I was going to use Paul's service on four one-ways that week. Upon arriving at the airport on the first leg, I asked Paul whether he could just process my Visa card for four trips that week and let his other drivers know that I was paid in full all week.

I will never forget how Paul responded. He said, repeating himself, "Patrick, you are the customer; of course, whatever you want, I can do for you. Whatever you need, I can make happen!" I dropped my jaw. His comments reaffirmed how special a person he was and that he was indeed an Affluent Entrepreneur ready to solve his customer's problems. He and his team continue to amaze me. He always goes the extra mile to do whatever the customer needs.

A year earlier, I had sat on the Bainbridge Island Lacrosse Board for our high school team. At that time, cutbacks had hit the school district, and we learned at the last minute that our JV lacrosse team (which plays its away games at 5 PM) would not be able to get school district bus service for our away games. Additionally, the other challenge was that many of the parents work during the day and can't get off work at 3 PM to drive their kids to the games. So after contemplating this quandary, we called some private busing companies in Seattle to get a price quote. Then we called Paul. You guessed it; he was more affordable and dependable than a private bus company. Roughly 20 to 25 JV lacrosse players got off the ferry in Seattle and jumped into three of Paul's stretch limos to and from the games on several occasions that season. The kids loved every bit of it, and it was no wonder that some of the other teams disliked Bainbridge lacrosse—not only are they envious of the team's state championships, but on several occasions, the team members have traveled in style to and from their games in stretch limos.

I share with you these stories because Paul and his company, Imperial Limousine, is a perfect example of an Affluent Entrepreneur scoping the marketplace in Seattle to search for a problem and then creating a venture to provide a solution. As a result, you can ask any adult living on Bainbridge Island how he gets to and from the airport and everyone will simply answer, "Paul, of course!"

I challenge you to do the same. Look for a problem in the marketplace, whether it is in your backyard or in the global community; then create a business with a product or service to provide the solution. When you carry out this simple process of due diligence, you successfully take the first step in eliminating your dependence on your day job and make progress toward becoming an Affluent Entrepreneur.

Do What You Are Good at and Enjoy

Next, take an inventory of your talents, your skills, and your god-given abilities. In doing so, you need to learn to recognize what you are good at and enjoy. During my many years of selling printed circuit boards, I enjoyed and was good at the selling part, but I didn't have a passion for how technology works. I don't care how it works; I just enjoy the results it provides. My discovery that I didn't have a passion for technology made it easier for me to transition full-time into my own business (for which I am passionate) after my layoffs in 2001 and 2002, as opposed to continuing to do something I did not enjoy.

What do you enjoy? What are you good at? How do you spend your free time during your evenings and weekends? If you won the lottery and money were no longer an issue, what would you do, and how would you spend your time? Chances are you can transform your passions into your profession. Find something you love to do where you can serve a need in the marketplace and then build your empire, your business, on this premise . . . and as a result, you will never have to work another day of your life.

I quit my job at age 36 on my own terms. Since then I have been traveling the world as an inspirational speaker, best-selling author, and publishing and book marketing coach. Yes, it is true, I do put in long hours, but I must say that I have not worked a day of my life in the last seven plus years. What I do is not work—it is fun; it is my passion; it is what I love to do.

As I write this book, I am approximately two-thirds of the way across the Pacific Ocean on a Cathay Pacific flight from Los Angeles to Hong Kong. After a short layover in Hong Kong, I will take another flight to Kuala Lumpur, Malaysia where I will be the featured keynote speaker at the Malaysia 2009 Sales and Money Conference. I will speak for six hours or so to 500 business owners and salespeople. Many of these attendees will become my good friends, clients, and business partners. I will get to see yet another beautiful part of the world and meet so many great people. Again I ask, *Is this work?* Absolutely not! It's a four-day minivacation to the other side of earth. Better yet, the organization that has hired me to speak is paying for my entire trip plus my speaking fee. I don't share this story with you to impress you, only to let you see that when you do what you love, and do what you enjoy, you can make a tremendous living and pursue the life of an Affluent Entrepreneur.

Another example I want to share with you comes from a college buddy of mine named Scot Engler. He and I attended the University of Montana together. He lived in the next dorm room over, and we hung out together for all four years of college. He was an incredible athlete and all around great guy. He played football for the Grizzlies before a knee injury ended his career.

Scot and several of my other buddies often (at least I thought so) seemed to waste a lot of time in college not studying. I remember them collecting baseball cards, playing fantasy baseball, video games, and always getting the newspaper tracking stats of their favorite baseball players. I thought Scot was wasting his great potential on his hobby when he could be doing something else that would help him to succeed in life. But little did I know he would become one of my most successful friends by doing exactly what he has always loved—baseball.

After a few odd jobs out of college, he landed an internship working with a pro baseball team. After working his way up in the ranks, he has been a pro baseball scout for the last 15 years. He has worked for the Montreal Expos, Florida Marlins, and now is a pro scout for the Texas Rangers. When I say pro scout, I mean that he only scouts players who are already in the major leagues. He makes his living do nothing more than watching pro baseball games, looking for talent, and making recommendations to his General Manager based on his observations and stats analysis in hopes of facilitating trades to improve the team's roster. A tough life—watching baseball, analyzing stats, and negotiating with agents. Sounds a lot like what he did in college. Boy, was I wrong. I always knew he was a great guy and was going to be successful, but I never knew how successful he would become just by doing what he loves. He truly is an Affluent Entrepreneur even though he has a job. How can I say this? Because he has a skill set he can apply to any team in professional baseball.

Again, I challenge you to do the same! Find something you love, something you have a god-given talent for and that you are good at, and something you enjoy; then build your business, your empire, around these talents. In doing so, you too will be on your way to becoming an Affluent Entrepreneur.

MOST MARKETABLE PASSIONS

The next step in the process is trying to select the one passion you have that you think will give you the best shot at achieving prosperity. If you are like most people, you have many, many talents and passions. The key is to evaluate each of these passions and find the one you think has the best chance of filling a need in the marketplace.

For example, I have a passion for the National Football League—so much so that as you may have read in my first book, *Creating Your Own Destiny*, I have a goal to own an NFL football team by age 50. My team either will be an expansion team called the Hawaii Tiger Sharks in Honolulu or I would like to purchase the Seattle Seahawks. We will talk more about that passion in a later chapter.

Over the years, I have come to grips with the fact that although owning my own NFL team is a major passion of mine, it is not the most marketable passion at the present time in my career. My most marketable passion is professional speaking, high-volume book sales, and publishing and book marketing coaching. I believe these are the vehicles to help me achieve my financial goals. If you study the current owners in the NFL (other than those who inherited their teams from their families), you will find that virtually all earned the seed money to purchase their teams outside of the NFL in other business ventures that were in alignment with their most marketable passions.

EXERCISE

I've shared these stories with you because I want you to soul-search. Write down a list of what you consider are your talents, what you enjoy, and how you want to spend your time. If you need more room than provided below, get out a separate sheet of paper.

What are my talents?

1. _____

2. _____

3. _____

4. _____

5. _____

What do I enjoy?

1. _____

2. _____

3. _____

4. _____

5. _____

How do I want to spend my time?

1. _____

2. _____

3. _____

4. _____

5. _____

Now go through those lists and circle the two things you think are the most marketable. Finally, do your research and determine which one of the two has the greatest opportunity for you to solve problems or needs in the marketplace. As a result of going through this process you will discover your most marketable passion.

UNIQUE SELLING PROPOSITION

When deciding what kinds of products or services to sell, it is important to ask yourself WHY people will buy your product or service instead of your competitor's. You need to determine what Doug Hall, author of *Jump Start Your Business Brain*, calls a "Unique Selling Proposition" so you can set yourself apart from the others.

For example, if you decide to sell calculators on the Internet, you had better come up with a darn good reason why people should buy *your* calculators since they could just as easily go to the local office supply store and pick one up the same day.

As a professional speaker and author, I try to set myself apart from the other speakers by advising the meeting planners that, when they pay my speaking fee, I also include several free copies of my book, *Creating Your Own Destiny*, and that I will cover all of my transportation costs and meals. (Most speakers will try to nickel-and-dime a meeting planner to death trying to get up-grades on flights, limo rides to and from the airport, as well as dining in expensive restaurants on their dime.) Because I cover all of these expenses and throw in copies of my book, meeting planners have a more enjoyable experience booking me to speak instead of my competition.

KEEPING YOUR OVERHEAD LOW

When starting a business, it is absolutely crucial to keep your expenses low. You need to be aware of numerous operating expenses, especially the ones that can be eliminated altogether.

EXERCISE

Think of one of your favorite companies and list three reasons why you buy from it instead of buying from its competition:

1. _____

2. _____

3. _____

Now write down three reasons why people will buy your product or service (these reasons become your Unique Selling Proposition):

1. _____

2. _____

3. _____

For example, many of you reading this book may have a one-person enterprise, or perhaps have a team of 10 people or less. Based on this size (unless you are a retail establishment) there is really no need for you to go out and lease office space, which can be a costly expense and is completely unnecessary. If you have an extra bedroom, garage, or anywhere in your residence with a door to shut out noise from the rest of the house, then you can set up your home office.

You will need a quiet area that has multiple outlets to plug in your computer, router, phone, printer, and so on. If you feel that you need a nice place to meet clients . . . take them out to a restaurant, coffee shop, or country club to conduct your meeting, but don't bring them to your residence if you feel your home office is not impressive. Your home office does NOT need to be impressive; it needs to be functional!

For years, I operated my business, The Snow Group, out of the comforts, or lack thereof, of my garage. Why my garage? Well, we lived in a three-bedroom, two-bath house, and each of my boys wanted his own room. I wanted to be somewhere away from the noise of a busy household where I could shut my door and have silence. I also needed a place where I could inventory all of my books and the ping-pong table provides ample countertop space for sending out preview books on a daily basis.

Five hundred dollars later in paint and added outlets, I had converted my garage into my home office. One of my close friends immediately named my home office "HQ" (for headquarters), and now everyone close to me knows where I am when I say I'm working at "HQ." If you have a team of business partners or employees, encourage them all to work out of their homes as well.

Save your money for marketing your business, because marketing directly returns revenues to your bottom line. Fancy office space does nothing more than give you unneeded extra stress each and every month while you worry about making your monthly lease payments. If you can keep your overhead low, you will be well on your way to becoming an Affluent Entrepreneur.

WRITING A BUSINESS PLAN

I saved the best for last. The most important thing you can do for your business is to write a business plan so you know how you are going to pull it all off. You may have it all in your head, which is a good start, but for a strong finish, you must have a business plan. Struggling Entrepreneurs don't have business plans; Affluent Entrepreneurs do. Struggling Entrepreneurs are broke; Affluent Entrepreneurs are prosperous. A business plan may come in many forms and doesn't need to be 30 to 40 pages. It can be as short as 10 to 15 pages. A major reason for your business plan is that you may need to raise seed money for your business, and investors will be more apt to give you money if they can see that you went through the process of writing a business plan.

I have written many, many business plans over the years. The first was for an entrepreneurship class in college for Dr. Paul Larsen at the University of Montana. This process was without question absolutely the most important experience I had at UM. It was here that I placed third as an undergraduate in an MBA graduate business plan competition (very good, considering I was an undergraduate studying political science).

There are many variations and components of a strong business plan. The style or formation you use does not really matter; what matters is that you actually create one and then follow it as you launch your venture. A detailed business plan needs to include the following:

Executive Summary. An Executive Summary is a one-page complete overview of your business model, proving that a need exists in the marketplace for your product or service. It also lists the owners/management team for your venture, offering their experience in your venture's industry. This page also gives a quick overview of the sales and marketing plan and finally a brief listing of competition and an implementation schedule.

Mission Statement. A Mission Statement is typically two to three paragraphs that describe why you are launching your business and what you hope to accomplish. Typically, here you would describe the level of experience you desire to give to your customer from your service and the benefits your customers will receive as a result of using your product.

Vision Statement. People sometimes think that a Vision Statement is the same as a Mission Statement, but there is definitely a difference. A Vision Statement is typically a one-page overview of what your company will look like 3 to 5 or maybe even 10 years down the road, including where your company will stand among its competition, its annual revenues, and the qualities of the products and services offered.

The Current Problem. The Current Problem is a detailed analysis of the market conditions as a result of performing due diligence, interviewing customers of the product or services, and interviewing other companies in the industry. This process is all about doing whatever you can to identify the problems in the current marketplace.

Your Solution. Your Solution is your company's overall solution and strategies to fix, solve, or improve the level of service that existing customers in the industry are experiencing. It is about providing a better, more enjoyable experience for the customer.

The Sales Strategy. The Sales Strategy is about the model you intend to use to market your company's product or service. For example, are you going to hire direct salaried employees to fill out your sales team? Are you going to go with some type of commission-based incentive for your representatives? Are you going to position your company using a direct sales model? Perhaps you are going to rely on referral selling or joint ventures. Also if not you, then who will be the people responsible for driving revenue to your bottom line?

The Marketing Strategy. The Marketing Strategy is all about how you are going to brand your product in the marketplace to determine the exact methods for launching your product or service. Are you going to spend money on advertising or implement more cost-effective marketing strategies?

Profit and Loss Cash Flow Analysis. Profit and Loss Cash Flow Analysis is about determining what your company's actual cash-flow needs are and how profits and revenues will be reinvested into the company. Part of this process is determining how much you as the owner draw out of the business as the owner and CEO.

The Competition. The Competition is about performing analysis of the strengths and weaknesses of your competitors to determine how your business can do a better job in service and pricing, as well as showing how your product or service is superior to your competitors' products and services.

The Challenges. The Challenges is all about determining which market forces are working against you, including overhead and operating expenses. Other challenges may include attracting seed money or investors to give you enough funding to ensure your success.

Implementation Schedule. The Implementation Schedule determines the timetable in which you launch your business model, bring in revenues, and determine what additional resources are purchased to reinvest in your business.

Key Points to Ensure Success. The Key Points to Ensure Success may be the most important part of this process, which will determine exactly what you need to ensure so no matter what the market conditions are, your business is a success.

As you can see, there are many components to writing a successful business plan. But most important, writing a business plan is the best way to give your company a shot at succeeding. Too many businesses fail, and when you get right down to determining the reasons for those failures, you will see that often many of them never took the time to actually write a business plan.

AFFLUENT ENTREPRENEUR PROFILE
FREDERICK WEYERHAEUSER

At 18 years of age, Frederick Weyerhaeuser emigrated from Germany to the United States and immediately began his career working in a sawmill. He eventually bought that sawmill and began purchasing others as well. In 1872, he launched the Mississippi Boom and Logging Company.

Weyerhaeuser went on in 1900 to purchase 900,000 acres of timberland in the Pacific Northwest from James J. Hill (a railroad baron) and founded The Weyerhaeuser Timber Company. He eventually acquired interests in Potlatch Corporation and Boise Cascade in Idaho. His strategy was to purchase millions of acres of land at undervalued prices and use the land for timber, sawmills, paper factories, and other such enterprises.

Talk about a "buy low and hold" real-estate investor— he was the real deal. He had discovered a rather unique product: millions of acres of land. And his unique selling proposition was this: He owned most of it—the timber, the mills, and the entire supply chain. Best of all, because Weyerhaeuser reforested, the timber would replace itself again completely over time without his ever having to cash in his chips and sell the land. He learned to take farming to another level altogether. As a result, Weyerhaeuser amassed a personal fortune of an estimated $72 billion (in 2006).

SUMMARY

Creating your own product or service that is unique to the market-place is an absolute must if you are to succeed in business. However, as important as finding the right product is, one thing even more important is to find a business that matches your passions and is marketable in today's economy.

To further drive this point home, I encourage you to read Marsha Sinetar's book *Do What You Love, The Money Will Follow*. I think her title pretty much describes what this process is all about. When you follow this advice, you will wake up each morning with a zeal for life, a desire to serve other people, and a mission to add value. As a result, you will thrive, create your own destiny, and become an Affluent Entrepreneur. And as an added bonus, you will never have to work another day in your life.

Conversely, if you rely on your current job to help you achieve your destiny, you may be severely disappointed in the years to come. Ask any baby boomer whether her job lasted forever, and you will quickly learn that jobs are nothing more than temporary vehicles to earn you seed money to build your business and become an Affluent Entrepreneur.

My concern and hope is that you do not get brainwashed into the trap of having a job and thinking that is the way to prosperity.

It is not! If you go down that route and don't save and invest enough money, eventually your funds will run out, and you will be forced to join hundreds of thousands of others who will desperately accept any job they can get and end up having to memorize the following, *"Would you like fries with your burger?"*

I challenge you to be inspired by Weyerhaeuser's story and create a unique product or service that can provide for your family for your lifetime, and for many generations to come.

Identifying Hot Trends in the Marketplace

> Any sufficiently advanced technology is
> indistinguishable from magic.
> —Arthur C. Clarke

I n the last chapter we talked about creating your own product or service that you can market to the world. In this chapter we are going to talk about ways you can judge whether your product or service is hot or not. The best way to make this determination is to keep an open mind, study trends in the marketplace, and then ask yourself whether people want to purchase the products or services you are offering or plan on offering. Additionally, you will learn how Cornelius Vanderbilt and others made a fortune by following their guts and riding the wave of a major trend in the transportation industry.

We all know things that were hot in the past but are no longer hot today. For example, CDs and CD duplication are now being replaced by video download. In other words, the technology used for creating the CD product for storage of content is soon going to be outdated just like vinyl records, eight-track tapes, cassette tapes, big box TVs, and typewriters. Desktop computers are being replaced by laptop computers, which are being replaced by smart phones and new technologies such as the Apple iPad.

As you look into the future, ask your teenagers what they see as hot products in the marketplace; chances are they will have an edge up on you since they are closer to the new and hip products of tomorrow.

In fact, I am sure this chapter will soon be outdated due to the new advances in technology right around the corner. Below are some items I firmly believe will continue to increase in popularity, so the question must be this: Are you keeping up with technology and trends or getting behind?

Telecommunications, wireless connections, social media, health care, transportation, technology, computers, cell phones, and other areas all have trends that continue to expand with no end in sight. All of these are hot today, and I believe they will continue to be strong trends for years to come. So ask yourself: *Does your product or service fit into any one of these categories?*

Investigating and studying the market to recognize what is hot will save you time and money because it will place your business in an industry with a proven record in a growing market. There's an old saying: "A rising tide lifts all boats." You want to get in on that rising tide! Through learning more about this principle, you'll be able to determine whether your product or service will sink or sail. As an entrepreneur, one of the most important skills you need is the ability to evaluate a business opportunity.

TREND OF COLLECTING GOLD AND SILVER COINS

Due to the recent real-estate and mortgage collapse and the loss of millions of dollars by investors, more and more people worldwide are diversifying their portfolios by purchasing gold and silver. These people are not just buying any form of these precious metals, but are buying them in the form of currency (collectible, minted gold and silver numismatic coins). *Numismatics* is the study and collecting of legal tender coins produced by the world's government mints.

The gold and silver collectible coins industry has grown into a $10 billion per year industry in the United States and a $100 billion industry worldwide. In years past if you did not know how to get started purchasing numismatic gold and silver coins, you may have been overwhelmed and not participated in this trend. However, today one company is pioneering the sale of graded silver and gold numismatic collectible coins. Numis Network (based in Tampa, FL) has made it easier than ever for you to get started in this trend and begin collecting minted numismatic gold and silver coins from government mints throughout the world. Numis' vision is to become the largest retailer in the world of certified and precious metal coins. Their goal is to help you create wealth, collect wealth, and preserve wealth.

For years Robert Kiyosaki, wealth guru and author of *Rich Dad Poor Dad*, has been preaching a diversification strategy of buying gold and silver as a way to protect yourself from the fluctuations of the dollar. What attracted me to Numis is that it is ahead of the curve by helping ordinary people not only to get started in collecting gold and silver graded numismatic coins, but it also has allowed and encouraged its customers to become part of this booming trend while actually earning money by introducing others to this industry and helping them to start their own collections. What a concept—earning money while collecting it! As a result, Numis Network only sells coins that have been certified by the largest and most trusted coin grading services including ANACS, NCG, and PCGS. For more information on this trend and to learn how you can start your collection of numismatic gold and silver coins, visit www.NumisNetwork .com/PatrickSnow.

MATCHING YOUR PASSIONS TO TODAY'S TRENDS

Combining your passions to the current trends of the time is so very important if you truly want to become an Affluent Entrepreneur. As an author, speaker, and coach, years ago I decided to pursue my passion in these industries not only because I love them, but also because they continue to grow year after year with no end in sight. Let me share with you some numbers that drive home this point. The Association of American Publishers estimated that in 2009, book sales reached $23.9 billion, and each year this number just keeps growing.[1] For that reason, I am in a growing business that is consistent with my passions. The American Society of Association Executives has estimated that the conference and meeting industry in the United States is $56 billion a year,[2] and these events require public speakers to attract attendees, so again I have a product to offer—myself as a public speaker. Finally, in 2006, the personal development industry was estimated to be at $8.9 billion a year; in 2010 it has reached over $19 billion with estimates that it will continue to grow as much as 50 percent annually.[3] I'm sure with numbers like these, you understand why I am in these industries that also provide me the opportunity to pursue my passions.

My point is this, match your passion with the trends of the day, and you will create a recipe for great wealth and career fulfillment, while at the same time providing a solution to a problem or need in the marketplace. When you do this, you will discover the key to spending the rest of your live living your passion, making great money, living your dream, and making a huge contribution to the world.

IDENTIFYING OTHER TRENDS BUT NOT WORKING IN THAT INDUSTRY

One of the key traits that Affluent Entrepreneurs possess is the ability to recognize opportunity and take quick action. Now this action doesn't necessarily mean that you yourself need to change completely your company's products or services to adapt to new trends in the marketplace. Bottom line is that these trends may

---

[1] www.publishers.org

[2] http://www.referenceforbusiness.com/industries/Service/Professional-Membership-Organizations.html

[3] David Allred, "$8.9 Billion Dollar Industry," at http://www.articleslash.net/Self-Improvement/186887__8-9-Billion-Dollar-Industry.html

be in a completely different industry—maybe even in an industry you are not qualified to participate in as a manufacturer or service provider.

But that doesn't mean you can't participate in this trend as an outside investor. What am I getting at? Well, you don't need to understand how all the circuitry, vias, traces, components, or chips all work together in harmony in order for you to recognize the upside potential of the iPad. The same is true with an iPod. If you enjoy customizing your own music with no annoying advertisements, then chances are other people will, too. Perhaps then, Apple would be a good company to invest in to diversify your portfolio.

A Personal Transportation Trend

One technology that has always fascinated me, although I can't comprehend it (perhaps because my degree is in political science), is the "flying car" industry. You may not be aware that we are closer than ever to having "flying cars" as part of our society. I am intrigued by this sector of the transportation industry for two reasons. First, I live on Bainbridge Island, Washington, and it is a 35-minute ferry ride to travel across the Puget Sound to arrive in Seattle. Second, I will soon have a second residence in Hawaii, meaning I will be distant from the outer islands I may need to visit.

I can't wait until I purchase and experience my first flying car so I can travel to Seattle by air in 5 to 10 minutes instead of 35 minutes by ferryboat. Furthermore, it will be very exciting to go island hopping in Hawaii with my second flying car parked in my garage at my vacation home. My point is this: You and I don't have to understand the technology behind the industry; what we need to understand is the buying habits of consumers in this industry to determine whether or not flying cars will take off as a trend. Let me share some insights with you on the evolution of this sector of the transportation industry.

Without question, the leading manufacturer and engineering firm in the world that is spearheading the effort to one day make the "flying car"—or Personal Air Vehicle (PAV) as it is better known in the industry—into a reality is Moller International (www .Moller.com), founded by Paul S. Moller and located in Davis, California.

I had the unique privilege of personally interviewing Dr. Moller by phone regarding this technology and the acceptance (or lack thereof) by large aircraft manufacturers and governments alike. Just as the case with the Wright Brothers in 1900 when inventing the first airplanes, the push-back in the PAV industry has been no different.

A quote on the Moller web site's home page says it all: "New technology goes through three stages: First it is ridiculed by those ignorant of its potential. Next it is subverted by those threatened by its potential. Finally, it is considered self-evident."

I asked Dr. Moller about the operator's ability to pilot such a vehicle. He responded, "In the future, the aircraft operators will not need to be pilots. They will simply know how to program a location by putting in their desired destination and letting the aircraft's computer system take over flying the PAV from point A to point B."

Next I asked him about the timing of production and how long it will take for these PAVs to be embraced and become a regular part of our society. Let's face it, I watched *The Jetsons* cartoon on TV growing up so I am eager to learn how close we are to seeing this technology as part of our everyday lives. His response was that he and Dan Goldin (former head of NASA) had testified a few years ago in front of a congressional hearing, and they both believe that "within ten years, 25 percent of the U.S. population will be able to afford to access the technology and within 25 years, 90 percent of the U.S. population will be able to access it." Something to keep in mind though is that when he says access it, it may mean that you either own one or you rent one for your convenience, similar perhaps today to renting a car.

Finally, I was interested, as any consumer would be, in cost. Currently, to manufacture one of the PAVs, you are looking at $500,000 or more, but eventually as this technology takes off, Moller's vision is that he will be able to price vehicles like these at around $100,000 or equivalent to what a high-end luxury automobile costs today.

As with any cutting edge, leading technology and continuous funding and investment are always part of the equation. Therefore, if you or someone you know is interested in this technology, feel free to contact a representative at Moller International for more specific details on investment options.

EXERCISE A

What are features of your product or service that address a rising trend today and in the future?

1. _____

_____

_____

2. _____

_____

_____

3. _____

_____

_____

EXERCISE B

What adjustments can you make in your business plan to ensure that what your product or service delivers will match the current and future trends in the marketplace?

1. _____

_____

_____

2. _____
   _____
   _____

3. _____
   _____
   _____

EXERCISE C

What trends can you identify that you know will continue? Which companies manufacture products or services that supply solutions to meet those trends? Which companies should you considering investing in to boost your net worth and benefit from the rising tide?

1. _____
   _____
   _____

2. _____
   _____
   _____
   _____

3. _____
   _____
   _____

AFFLUENT ENTREPRENEUR PROFILE
CORNELIUS VANDERBILT

Cornelius Vanderbilt was an American entrepreneur who recognized the trend and increased demand for transportation in a pioneering America. Born on Staten Island, New York, in 1794, he grew up working on his father's ferryboat, which operated runs between Manhattan and Staten Islands. He quit school at age 11, operated his own boat by age 16, and soon thereafter, purchased the ferryboat with borrowed money. These experiences led him into a long and prosperous career in shipping, and eventually, he bought out all of the other ferry lines operating in the lower Hudson River area.

In the 1830s, some of the first railroads were being built between Boston and Long Island Sound, where they connected with steamboats to make the remaining portion of the trip to New York City. It didn't take long before Vanderbilt owned these railroads as well. When the California Gold Rush started in 1849, he switched his attention from regional steamboat lines to ocean-going steam ships. Virtually all of the migrant workers heading out West, and all the gold coming back to the East, traveled on Vanderbilt's ships by way of Panama.

After the Civil War, Vanderbilt turned his attention back to the railroad industry, where he soon ran into conflicts with connecting railroads. He solved the problem by buying them out; soon he owned the Hudson River Railroad, New York Central Railroad, Lakeshore and Michigan Southern Railway, and later the Canada Southern. Vanderbilt was also the driving force behind Grand Central Depot on 42nd Street in Manhattan in 1871, now called Grand Central Station.

As a result of his acquisitions over the years in both the shipping and railroad industries, at the time of his death in 1877, Cornelius Vanderbilt amassed a net worth valued at $100 million, which in 2007 dollars would be worth $143 billion. He would go on to make a huge endowment, which would result in Vanderbilt University in Nashville, Tennessee, being named in his honor.

SUMMARY

To become an Affluent Entrepreneur, you need to keep your pulse on the trends in the marketplace. Whenever possible, try to match your passions with these trends and then create a product or service capable of providing solutions and solving problems with this trend. In doing so, you will create great wealth and amass a fortune.

Whether it be Cornelius Vanderbilt in shipping and railroads, Henry Ford with automobiles, the Wright Brothers in airplanes, or Paul Moller with PAVs (flying cars), be sure that you study the demand in the marketplace and then position yourself and your company to rise with the incoming tide that lifts all ships.

Better yet, if you are not in a position to offer products or services to these "trendy" industries, consider positioning yourself as an investor to diversify your portfolio. By becoming an investor, you can save time by following your true passions, while not having to spend years and years trying to understand the technology. Save that for the engineers.

Getting Your Family's Support

The most important thing a father can do for his
children is to love their mother.
—Henry Ward Beecher

In this chapter, you will learn how crucial it is to get your family's
support on your venture. We are not talking about extended
family. We are not talking about Mom and Dad, Brother and
Sister; we are talking about your spouse. From the start, even *before*
the start, you must include your family in your business. After all,
think about what you're going to put them through! While you're
visualizing how you'll spend your first million, your family is afraid
of the unknown. Tell your husband or wife everything. Your
spouse needs to know what you're planning, what he or she should
expect, and any sacrifices your family will have to make.

For example, your spouse needs to know there won't be a
guaranteed paycheck every week, no eight-hour workdays, and that
your family's credit score may take a big hit. Your family needs to
commit to supporting and encouraging you in this new venture for
five to seven years. If they make this sacrifice, then they'll benefit
from the pot of gold at the end of the rainbow that follows every
storm. Getting your spouse's support may mean the difference
between success and failure in your business. It almost goes
without saying—family support is essential.

Additionally, in this chapter you will learn how the wealthiest
man in the world, Bill Gates, included his wife in his business
model and why you also need to keep your spouse involved.

CREDIT SCORE

The two words above are probably the single two biggest road-blocks that prevent people from pursuing their dreams. A credit score paralyzes people with fear. Why? Because we are taught early on that the single most important thing in life is to keep a "perfect" credit score. I was taught that as well. Well, let's probe this idea a bit further. The reason why people want a perfect credit score is so they can one day pursue the American Dream: buy a house (debt), buy a car (debt), and secure a good education for their kids (usually also means debt).

The reason why I find this belief so humorous is that I too shared this philosophy for so many years. I had a perfect credit score of over 800 when I was laid off at 9/11, and then I started investing heavily into my own business. Once I lost the six-figure day job, I got behind on bills and hence no longer had a perfect credit score. Banks will make you believe that if your credit score is below 600, you are not a good person—you are a bad person, a failure.

I have come to believe that is all a bunch of bullshit! Recent studies suggest that 55 percent of American adults (over 110 million) have bad credit. Who cares? As far as I am concerned, it is just a number. Today, bad credit is as common as having blue eyes or being born on an odd day of the month. I could care less what your credit score is. I am more concerned with the goodness of your heart than the number on your credit report. What a dinged credit score tells me is that you are an entrepreneur, a risk taker, a visionary, and someone who is trying to build and create something for the greater good of all humanity. I do care about your visions, your goals, your destiny, and your higher calling in life. Those are things far more important to me when considering whether I choose to do business with someone. I am sure if you were to ask all of the entrepreneurs alive today about their credit history, they too would admit that it has been up and down over the years.

What I mean is that your credit score has nothing to do with who you are as a person, your level of success or failure in the future, or whether you are a caring, forgiving, honest, contributing member of society. The opposite is true . . . perhaps having a lower credit score means that you have dreams, that you took action, that the successes didn't come as quickly as you anticipated, so you ended up getting behind on your bills a little bit. Big deal! In the end, you become an Affluent Entrepreneur worth millions, and hire all those people with perfect credit scores to work for you while you sit on the beach or travel the world and build your empire. Donald Trump has filed bankruptcy as a business strategy. Do you think he has a perfect credit score?

In truth, your credit score does not mean a damn thing if you pay cash for all of your purchases! It is just a number, just like your Social Security or driver's license number. Who cares what the number is if you have all the cash in the world at your disposal. Furthermore, having good credit just gives you the ability to borrow money to buy things you cannot afford to buy without cash, leaving you further in debt. For example, if you make good money and have a perfect credit score, you can go out and get a car loan and buy an $80,000 Mercedes Benz; now sure you have a nice car, but you are stuck with $80,000 in debt and a monthly payment of $1,000.

Another example: You are making good money and have a perfect credit score, so you go out and purchase a million-dollar home; now you live in a nice home, but you are stuck with an $7,500 per month mortgage payment. More debt, less freedom!

My point is that while you should do everything you can to meet your financial obligations, pay all of your bills on time, and keep a decent credit score, don't feel that if your credit has been dinged, you are a failure. You are not. The systems that track credit are actually protecting you from buying things you really can't afford and keeping you from getting more in debt.

Bottom line, the Affluent Entrepreneur is one who pays cash for everything and only truly buys things he needs! There are two exceptions to this rule: One, he can use OPM (other people's money) as a tool to buy the things he needs, wants, or desires; and two, the Affluent Entrepreneur borrows money to purchase appreciating assets such as real estate.

COMING TO TERMS WITH YOUR SPOUSE

When you or your spouse are thinking of starting a business or getting into business with someone else, make sure that one of the two of you keeps her nose to the grindstone and keeps the day job. What I mean is that it will not work in many cases if both the husband and the wife are pursuing new ventures simultaneously.

One of you should keep your job, while the other one is freed up to pursue the business. However, do what you can to ensure that all of your family's needs will be met with that one income. In doing so, either you or your spouse will have the extra time and energy to build a business while the other keeps their job. Perhaps you don't read about it in books or see it in the movies, but the most successful entrepreneurs are the ones who kept their family intact in both times of scarcity and abundance.

I remember how challenging things were after I was laid off from my high-tech sales job and I started making the transition to full-time business owner. At times, it was very difficult for our family to watch our perfect credit score get dinged, but my family has always been there, supporting my career pursuits every step of the way. I remember a conversation I had with my father when I was explaining how challenging things got financially when I lost my job after 9/11.

My father looked me in the eyes and said, "Fight like hell to keep your family together; it is the most important thing in the world!" I will never forget his words of wisdom. Today, of all my accomplishments in life, I am most proud of the fact that my family has always been there to support my entrepreneurial pursuits.

At one point early on in our transition, I got behind on our mortgage payments. So much so that my family and I ultimately had a "Come to Jesus" talk. We had been living in our family home for about eight years at the time. Unbeknownst to me, my family was tired of the house. So we decided to sell our home, take the money from it, and pay off all of our credit card debt. We did just that, and then we found a beautiful home on the golf course; it was a one-story rambler within walking distance to the beach and the ferry. Also because it was on the golf course, it was a very quiet place to live. We couldn't afford to buy it right away, so we did a lease option on the home, and within two years, we finally purchased it. We eventually sold the golf course home and now live in a new oceanfront penthouse condo on the south end of Bainbridge Island. Through the process, I have learned the secret to a happy family. That secret, if applied to your relationship, will make for many, many more happy years to come. It is simply that a happy family equals a happy life.

HAPPY FAMILY EQUALS HAPPY FUTURE

Have you ever found yourself in a position where your spouse continues to give you a "Honey-Do List"? Well, in my family, it is no different. My favorite is when I am watching an NFL game on TV and one of my family members comes up with some project to do, such as cleaning the fridge or some other painstaking task around the house.

Well, after we purchased our rambler on the golf course, we learned that, as a result of the frequent use of the fireplace, the chimney needed to be cleaned to eliminate the creosote build-up on its inside. I had never cleaned a chimney before, and I certainly did not have the tools, time, or energy to complete such a task. For months and months, my family was constantly after me to get it done. And because we were living on a budget, a chimney sweep just wasn't in my financial plan. See, all along I assumed it would cost $500 to $1,000 to get the job done.

Several months went by, and I still had not completed this item on the "Honey-Do List." As a result, I was always extra careful when making a fire in the fireplace. On January 16, 2007, it was my son Jacob's twelfth birthday, and he invited five boys over to spend the night. Being the good dad I was, I ordered several pizzas for the boys. I hung out with the boys in the family room where the fireplace is located and watched them play video games. Finally around midnight, I decided I should probably clean up the mess since it would be nice to wake up the next morning to a clean home. I picked up the leftover pizza boxes and took them outside to the garbage; wouldn't you know it, the round garbage can was full. And even if it hadn't been full, it would not hold a square pizza box. I've always thought pizza boxes should be made round to fit into garbage containers, or garbage cans should be made square to fit pizza boxes.

Being the rocket scientist I am, I decided to go back inside with the pizza boxes and simply throw them in the fire and watch them burn. Problem solved. Well, not so fast. Before I disposed of the three or four pizza boxes in the fireplace, I let my yellow Lab finish off any extra pizza toppings still left in the box. In doing so, I couldn't help but notice how much grease there was left on the pizza box. Having taken chemistry in both high school and college, I should have known better than to toss the greasy boxes into the fireplace, but I tossed them in anyway. I was amazed by what happened next.

To my surprise, after a few short moments of watching the boxes burn, I suddenly heard, "Thump. Thump. Thump." It sounded like the plastic container at a bank drive-thru as you send it back to the teller. Yes, you guessed it; a similar process happened with the pizza boxes. They were being sucked up the chimney. I prayed they would burn quickly without causing a problem.

Then, I heard the chimney start to roar. It got louder and louder, as if I were standing at the end of an aircraft carrier listening to the planes prepare for takeoff. I leaned over, put my head as close to the fire as I could, looked up the chimney, and saw that the entire top of the chimney was on fire. Boy, did I wish I had invested in a chimney sweep at that moment.

Meanwhile, the boys were all still playing video games, completely oblivious to the ever-increasingly dangerous situation. The others remained asleep in their bedrooms on the other side of the family room. So I rushed outside as fast as I could to assess the situation. Once I got out into the front yard, I looked up at the roof to see what appeared to be miniature Fourth of July fireworks spewing forth from the top of my chimney.

I realized now that my house's chimney was completely on fire. For a moment, I thought the obvious solution was to call 911. But that would waken my family, and I would hear grief from them for years to come about how I didn't get a chimney sweep as they had requested on the "Honey-Do List" for the past several months. The last thing I wanted was for my family to wake up and for my foolish actions to ruin Jacob's birthday party.

So I did what any guy who had not listened to his family would have done. I ran as fast as I could back into the house and grabbed the ladder and a hose. I turned on the hose, rushed to the side of the house, and then climbed up the ladder with the hose. I sprayed and sprayed water all over the top of the chimney and into the chimney. After three or four minutes, I had succeeded in putting out the chimney fire. Then I stayed up on the roof to hose everything down for another five minutes while grimacing from how badly the burnt pepperoni pizza boxes smelled.

When I was sure the fire was out and would not start back up, I rushed back into the house, fully expecting to find the water that came down the chimney all over the place. To my surprise, there was no water anywhere—it had all evaporated in the fireplace's flames. Furthermore, my son and his friends had remained so involved in their video game that they had no clue there had even been a chimney fire. I figured if they hadn't seen it, there was no reason for me to mention it, so I left them to continue enjoying the birthday party and video game.

Being the responsible father I am, I snuck into the bedroom, and I went into the closet to access the pull down attic ladder. Just as I did so, my other son rolled over and asked, "What is that god-awful smell?" I replied, "One of the boys must have burnt some pizza in the microwave." He quickly went back to sleep while I climbed up into the attic with my flashlight to rule out any chance of a new fire starting up in the attic. What I discovered was that our fireplace was completely encased in large stone, so it would be virtually impossible for fire to get into the attic. I went back downstairs then, snuck out of the bedroom, and went back to the family room where I let the fire in the fireplace naturally burn itself out—I was certainly not going to add any more wood to the fire.

By now it was 1 AM, and the boys were getting ready to sleep on the family room floor in their sleeping bags. Being a responsible father, while the boys slept I stayed up in the family room watching SportsCenter. Three hours later, with everyone soundly asleep, I knew the risk and danger were virtually eliminated so I went to bed.

The next day being Sunday, we had a fire again in our fireplace as we cheered on the Seahawks on the big screen TV. (After all, I couldn't not build a fire and let anyone suspect what had happened. I was a bit nervous about building the fire, but fortunately, the previous night's incident was not repeated.) Finally, Monday morning I immediately went to the yellow pages, looked up chimney sweep, and found AAA Chimney Sweeps. (By the way, that is a brilliant name because it ensured the company top alphabetical placement in the yellow pages.) I called the company, set up an appointment, and by that afternoon, they had come out and spent two hours completely cleaning out our entire chimney and getting rid of all of the creosote. Then the representative gave me the bill: $99.00.

That was it! I couldn't believe it. All that time spent worrying about where I was going to find another $1,000 in our family budget. I had risked the health and safety of my family and my son's friends for a mere $99.00. I felt like an idiot!

I share this story with you for this reason: What items are there on your "Honey-Do List" that your spouse has been after you about for months and months? I challenge you to respect your spouse and do what he or she has asked you to do! That's the least your spouse deserves when you consider all the support he or she will give you to become an Affluent Entrepreneur.

EXERCISE

In the lines below, list five things you can do for your spouse immediately (within the next five to seven days) to show that you love and respect your spouse so much you are willing to do anything to keep him or her happy!

1. _____

   _____

   _____

2. _____

   _____

   _____

3. _____

   _____

   _____

4. _____

   _____

   _____

5. _____

   _____

   _____

FAMILY MUST BE YOUR TOP PRIORITY

I remember several years ago in my early days of studying wealth, I read an article in *Reader's Digest* that listed the top reasons why many people never achieve wealth. One of the top reasons was divorce. Let's face it; when you are married, you are paying one mortgage or rent payment, one cable bill, one Internet bill, one power bill, one homeowner's bill, one tax bill, and the list goes on and on.

Once divorced, both you and your ex-spouse now need to cover all of the bills individually and with half the income you previously had as a family. The money aspect is still just the small part of the difficulties. There's the issue of the children. Where will they live? How will they respond? What long-term detrimental effects and scars are they left with due to Mom and Dad splitting up? I can't tell you how many adult friends I have today who have a screw or two loose, and when digging deeper into their personality and early years, they all describe how their parents' divorce messed them up for five years or more.

Affluent Entrepreneurs keep family as their top priority; they do not cheat on their spouses or abandon their children. The Affluent Entrepreneur does what my father encouraged me to do during my family's tough financial years: "Fight like hell to keep your family together!" As an entrepreneur, the most important product you bring to this world is your family. It doesn't matter how successful you are in business if you are not successful with your family!

For this reason, I am grateful to have successfully raised two wonderful sons. God willing, I am excited that someday my boys will have families of their own. I am so proud of my boys, Sam and Jacob, and of the young men they are becoming.

Recently, I read another book by one of my all-time favorite authors and speakers, Og Mandino. In *The Choice*, he concludes that we all have a choice in life. We have a choice to be faithful to our spouses, a choice to keep our children as a top priority, and a choice in business to be our own successful entrepreneur. Og states that having a happy family is like experiencing a "premature heaven on earth."

EXERCISE

In the space below, insert your spouse's name and commit that you will keep your spouse as a top priority in your life, meet his or her needs, and also share with him or her your entrepreneurial pursuits so your spouse will know what to expect, and what to sacrifice so you may ultimately achieve the light at the end of the tunnel. Notice that there is room for only one person's name here:

1. _____

Next, list your children below, and commit the rest of your life to keeping them as a top priority.

1. _____

2. _____

3. _____

4. _____

5. _____

In this chapter, I have written about the importance of keeping your family as a top priority. If you desire to become an Affluent Entrepreneur, you must commit with all of your heart and soul to remain faithful to your spouse and to be there for your children.

You must also remain firm and grounded in times of prosperity and turbulence. You must come to understand the power of paying cash for everything, and if you can't pay cash, you must understand that it means you don't purchase it (unless it is an appreciating asset such as real estate).

You should also never let someone else's opinion of you determine your self-worth. Know that part of the process of becoming an Affluent Entrepreneur means that at times your credit score will become damaged. Remember that having a dinged credit score actually helps to prevent you from borrowing money to purchase things you can't afford because you can't pay cash for them.

I challenge you to pursue your biggest passions in business, remain loyal and faithful to your spouse, and keep your children a top priority. When you do this, you will see that the other principles in this book will serve as your aid to achieve all of your family goals.

AFFLUENT ENTREPRENEUR PROFILE
BILL GATES

Bill Gates has become one of the best-known entrepreneurs in the world after he and cofounder Paul Allen launched Microsoft in 1975. He has completely revolutionized the computer industry and dominated the software industry from the 1980s to the present.

Mr. Gates has served as founder and CEO of Microsoft. In January 2000, he stepped down as CEO, but he has remained involved as Chairman of the company. As a result of his technological know-how and ruthless competitiveness, Bill Gates has amassed a personal fortune of $53 billion. His net worth was as high as $121 billion a few years ago at the height of Microsoft's stock value.

In 1994, during a booming time for the company, Gates began to study the philanthropic endeavors of Andrew Carnegie and John D. Rockefeller. Their example inspired him to create the William H. Gates Foundation, which was renamed in 2000 as the Bill and Melinda Gates Foundation. He decided to include his wife in the foundation since she has a stunning resume of accomplishments in her own right. Soon after the foundation's establishment, the Gates's were successful in recruiting fellow billionaire Warren Buffett to become involved in the foundation. Today, Bill Gates, his wife Melinda Gates, and billionaire friend Warren Buffett control the foundation as the three trustees.

The vision of this foundation is to enhance health care, reduce extreme poverty, expand educational activities, and improve access to information technology. The foundation has been quite successful in accomplishing this vision to make a difference throughout the world by giving $33 billion to the endowment to support its worldwide causes.

SUMMARY

Sooner or later, every entrepreneur learns that family is always more important than money. My goal in this chapter was to help you understand how to communicate with your spouse to gain his or her support in your entrepreneurial ventures. Let's face it; being an Affluent Entrepreneur without the love of your family by your side is ultimately a sign of failure.

Keep your spouse in tune with the risks at hand, and warn him or her if financial storms are soon to come. Finally, reward your spouse's loyalty to you and your vision once the storm has passed and life gets back to normal. Every entrepreneur is sooner or later going to deal with financial ups and downs, and the more you include your spouse in this rollercoaster, the stronger your marriage will be. The stronger your marriage, the stronger your relationship will be with your children.

As your business grows and succeeds, if your spouse is a willing participant, you may decide to include your spouse as part of your business (if it makes sense to). I am inspired by how Bill and Melinda Gates have come together as a family and as a foundation to make the world a better place. I challenge you to do the same by taking part of your profits and giving them back to those in need so you can do your part to create a greater good here on earth.

Applying the Principles of Successful Selling

Don't judge each day by the harvest you reap,
but by the seeds you plant.
—Robert Louis Stevenson

I n this chapter you will learn many of the skills to drive large revenues to your company, which will ultimately help you to become an Affluent Entrepreneur. You will learn the Affluent Entrepreneur's ultimate Sales Success Formula, which I believe is one of the most important equations sales professionals can use to produce amazing results. Next, you will learn 12 proven prospecting strategies. Finally, you will gain insight into how the top-performing IBM salesman, Ross Perot, became a billionaire.

STARTING YOUNG

Let's face it, becoming an Affluent Entrepreneur is not going to happen overnight. I believe Affluent Entrepreneurs are developed over time through hard work, trial and error, and sure determination. In other words, Affluent Entrepreneurs are not born—they are grown and nurtured. The best way you can ensure that your children will become Affluent Entrepreneurs is to cut them off financially and teach them to fish for themselves as early as possible, ideally in their mid- to late teens as my parents did with me.

When I was a young child, my parents told me that I could have anything I wanted so long as I was willing to work hard enough for it and also pay for it myself. This knowledge sent me on a journey as a young boy to mow grass, shovel driveways, and eventually, to sell *Detroit Free Press* subscriptions door-to-door and get a paper route in the eighth grade. It was the paper route that taught me how to collect money from my clients. I would argue that collecting money might be the absolutely most important skill an Affluent Entrepreneur needs to master. The second skill that is arguably equally important is selling! In this chapter we will cover selling from perhaps a different perspective from anything you have ever imagined. Remember, people love buying but hate being sold.

Let's begin this chapter with the obvious: You, the owner of your company, wear many hats. You are the president, CEO, operations manager, VP of sales, director of customer service, accountant, and collections officer. Oh yeah, I forgot—you are also the IT guy or gal and the janitor! Wearing lots of hats can cause you to lose focus on the number one most important function of your business, which is to drive revenues to your company. The only way you can do so is to focus at least half of your time on selling, prospecting, and bringing in revenue. This chapter is designed to help you become more effective at selling, closing business deals, and attracting clients to your business so you can become an Affluent Entrepreneur.

THE AFFLUENT ENTREPRENEUR'S SALES SUCCESS FORMULA

As an entrepreneur, you know what you want, but you may not know how to get it. No doubt, you're trying to start a new business or grow your existing one. During this process, some business owners fall into the trap of spreading themselves too thin, thus needing to increase their revenue. You may have the same concern.

Let's face it: Until your company adds more employees, you're wearing all those hats I already mentioned, and with all of those roles, how can you focus on the amount of prospecting needed to keep your revenue stream coming in? It's my belief that you can't until you implement a system specifically designed to keep you on track.

Becoming an Affluent Entrepreneur doesn't happen overnight. You'll face adversity, your bank account may run dry, and your perfect credit rating may suffer. You may damage your relationship with your spouse or significant other. In the end, your trials will be worth the pain if you can develop the courage to stay the course and make it happen!

You may be thinking, *Easier said than done.* Perhaps you've had a goal, a dream, or a vision that you didn't pursue because you didn't know how you could attain that goal. Many others have the same concerns. I'm going to offer you a system to follow so you can learn the "how." Once you unleash this secret, your business can explode.

Over the course of 15 years, I've interviewed thousands of employees from all walks of life. What do these people say they want? *More* time, *more* money, *more* freedom, *more* health, *more* love, and *more* happiness in life. Entrepreneurs want the same things, and when you own your own business, you're in a great position to achieve them!

Your ability to sell is vital to the level of success or failure you'll experience. The better your sales skills are, the more money you'll make. If you have a background in sales, then you're more qualified than you realize to succeed as an entrepreneur. Bottom line: Great salespeople make the best entrepreneurs.

So, how can an entrepreneur get more out of life? By overcoming self-limiting beliefs, applying the following sales success formula, and implementing my prospecting system.

YOUR BIGGEST OBSTACLE

Before I offer you my formula, it's important to identify your self-limiting beliefs. Your biggest obstacle isn't another company or entrepreneur, but you. Your mind can help or hurt you, depending on how you've programmed it. Rather than focusing on doubts, you must learn to believe and trust in yourself.

The best way to develop a strong belief in yourself is to set small, attainable goals. As you execute these goals, you'll learn you're capable of overcoming your self-doubt, enabling you to achieve more far-reaching goals.

Once you win the mind battle, you can accomplish all you envision. Your mind will ignite a fire in your heart. As you experience this success, you'll build your confidence until you become an unstoppable force, capable of achieving more success and freedom than you could have ever imagined.

THE FORMULA

It's important to analyze why people purchase products and services from one company over another. If you ask buyers, most say, "strong relationships." People buy from people they like. If you want to increase sales, you need to develop more solid relationships. The entrepreneur who becomes the person others want to do business with will ultimately get the biggest results.

Here's the Sales Success Formula I suggest you use:

Trust (T) + Respect (R) + Need (N) + *Ask* (A) = Money ($)

Like every formula, each part must be fulfilled to reach the desired outcome. Trust is crucial in order to close sales. Your prospect may respect your company, and he may have a need, but if he doesn't trust you, he won't buy from you.

To build trust, show your prospect you care about his success. When a buyer sees you care, then he'll trust you. The best way to earn this trust and respect is to let your prospect share his problems with you.

Another way to build trust in the relationship is to ask the buyer about his or her interests. Questions can include asking about his or her family, children, and hobbies. Asking these questions will give you a better idea of the buyer's interests, passions, and priorities.

Respect is another key component to this equation. It's possible to trust someone but not respect him. The best way to build respect is to follow up on action items as promised. Always respond in a timely manner. Show the prospect you value his business.

All too often, entrepreneurs forget to ask whether there's a need for their services or products. It's vital to qualify need as quickly as you can. Without it (regardless of how much trust and respect you've established), you'll never close the sale. To discover a prospect's need, ask whether he's in the market for your product or service. If not, move on to the next prospect and qualify that person's need.

PROSPECTING SYSTEM

In my business, I've had incredible months of growth and record income, while at other times I've struggled. Looking back at this rollercoaster ride, the worst months occurred when I spent a disproportionate amount of time doing administrative tasks. When I implemented my Sales Success Formula, I had my best months. I can't emphasize how important my system is to an entrepreneur. If you follow a proven system, you'll soar. If you don't, you'll starve. "SYSTEM" stands for: Save Your-Self Time, Energy, and Money. As an entrepreneur, I challenge you to implement the 12 tips in my prospecting system, listed below.

1. *Develop a sales database that works for you.* Numerous sales tools and CRM software applications are on the market that can help you keep in touch with your prospects. If you're old-school and prefer using a paper system, then do what works best for you. The less time you spend doing data entry, the more time you can prospect.

2. *A successful business is 5 percent creation and 95 percent daily promotion.* The old adage of "build it and they will come" doesn't work! Just because you create a new product, service, or web site, doesn't mean customers will come knocking on your door. Develop your product or service, then spend the rest of your life promoting it, and you'll experience success.

3. *Prospect a minimum of four hours per day.* Entrepreneurs can lose focus on their most important task: selling. Prospect four hours per day, and you'll bring in the revenue needed to thrive while you're also doing new product development.

4. *Utilize the rule of seven.* Studies show on average that it takes seven bits of communication between buyer and seller before a sale occurs. In today's ultracompetitive environment, the "one-call sales close" no longer works. You have to develop trust, respect, and need, which result from spending time with your prospect. After five or six communications, ask your prospect to become your client, and you'll have a high rate of success.

5. *Get samples in the hands of your prospects.* Many aspiring authors have asked me how I turned my book *Creating Your Own Destiny* into an international bestseller. It all came down to my willingness to give out review copies to prospects who would later buy my book in volume. I've given away an estimated 3,500 copies in 10 years. Focus on giving away samples of your product and then sell to the same clients in volumes of 10,000 units or more.

6. *Build a full-commissioned sales team.* As an entrepreneur, you must do everything possible to keep your overhead low. One of the best ways is to pay your team based on sales and project-specific performance, and not on salary (with the exception of administrative personnel).

7. *Create and update an income funnel.* You need to know from where your next paycheck is coming. Monitor all your prospects as they move through your sales funnel. This strategy allows you to manage your monthly cash flow.

8. *Focus on marketing your business instead of advertising.* It's been my experience that advertising can be costly and often doesn't work. Marketing your business is less expensive and more effective. For example, instead of paying the steep price of a newspaper ad, submit an article. This method costs you nothing, and sets you up as an expert in the eyes of your prospect.

9. *Protect your seed money sources.* A good form of seed money is income from your job. If you're just beginning your entrepreneurial pursuits, keep your day job and build your business part time. Once you have a year's worth of income saved and are debt free, then quit your job and pursue your venture full time.

10. *Successful businesses always take longer and cost more than planned.* It may take three times longer and cost three times more than you budgeted to make your business a success. Keep this in mind when allocating funds. This principle also helps you to determine how long you'll need to keep your job.

11. *Golden rule.* Simply put, treat others as you wish to be treated. Respect others as you wish to be respected. Prospect others as you wish to be prospected. Finally, sell others as you wish to buy.

12. *Negotiations.* Always remember that when it comes to negotiations, whoever mentions the amount first always loses. Therefore, let the other person or organization you are negotiating with bring up price first. In doing so, you will always be sure to get what you need for your product or service.

If you want to create your own destiny using the business you've selected as your financial vehicle, I challenge you to apply my Sales Success System to your business and follow my destiny mantra, "Dream, Plan, Execute, and Soar!"

How do you achieve your vision of success? The answer is a secret I've learned during my years as an entrepreneur: You *don't* need to know the "how." If you believe in your vision, the how will present itself over time. W. Clement Stone said, "If you tell enough other people about your goals and dreams, eventually someone in your life will show up and help you achieve them!"

EXERCISE

List five new sales and prospecting strategies below that you plan on implementing immediately to drive increased revenues to your company.

1. _____
   _____
   _____

2. _____
   _____
   _____

3. _____
   _____
   _____

4. _____
   _____
   _____

5. _____
   _____
   _____

AFFLUENT ENTREPRENEUR PROFILE
ROSS PEROT

Ross Perot graduated from the United States Naval Academy in 1953, served his remaining four years, and left the Navy to become a salesman for IBM in 1957. He quickly became the top-selling producer of his company, achieving his annual sales goals within the first two weeks.

This experience gave him the wisdom and the resources to launch his own company, Electronic Data Systems (EDS), in 1962. After 77 rejections, Ross Perot finally landed EDS contracts with the federal government to computerize medical records. His company eventually went public in 1968, and his stock value increased from $16 a share to $160 per share in a matter of a few days. The success of his company eventually led to GM purchasing the company for $2.4 billion.

Ross Perot developed what every good salesperson needs to possess: good listening skills. And he was persistent and never gave up. After listening to the numerous problems faced by the United States with its ever-increasing national deficit, Perot wanted to apply business principles to political problems. As a result, he had unsuccessful runs for president of the United States in both 1992 and 1996. It was in 1992 that I had the opportunity to meet him in person on one of his political campaigns. Being the true sales professional, he was a man I trusted and believed could do the job our country needed. I believed in him so much that he earned my vote.

As a result of a lifetime of listening to the problems of both the business marketplace and politics, Ross Perot built himself an empire. At a time when he could have

(continued)

(*continued*)
retired permanently, he spent his own money to go out on a limb in another attempt to serve the United States. As a result of his true professionalism, solid character, and salesmanship, Ross Perot amassed a net worth of $3.5 billion.

SUMMARY

I encourage you to implement my sales formula, $T + R + N + \underline{A} = \$$, to develop solid relationships based on trust, respect, and need, and then to ask the prospect for his or her business. Remember the *A* for "Ask" is always underlined because it is the most important part of the equation. My friend and mentor Mark Victor Hansen, coauthor of the record-breaking *Chicken Soup for the Soul* book series has always said, "You need to A-S-K to G-E-T!"

Becoming unstoppable and earning more money as an entrepreneur than you could have ever imagined is certainly within reach when you take the strategies outlined in this chapter and apply them to your business. As a result of implementing them, you'll ultimately get *more* out of life. It's my firm belief you must have unwavering confidence in yourself. Only those who can see the invisible can achieve the impossible. Belief in your vision is the key to creating your own destiny (but only if you go out there and do it yourself). Your ship is not going to come in; you need to leave the security of shore and swim out to it.

I challenge you to study the business and political life of Ross Perot, so you will learn firsthand and see a living example of someone who has applied the principle of successful selling to business and become an Affluent Entrepreneur as a result.

Finding and Hiring the Right People

Determine that the thing shall be done
and then we shall find a way.
—Abraham Lincoln

It's logical to want to attract winners to your team. In this chapter, I will help you develop the most logical, least risky compensation plan for your team. You will learn how to put this kind of compensation plan together: namely, a commission-only payout, meaning your teammates earn income only if they add revenue to your company's bottom line. Next, I will show you how and where to find this talent to help you build your empire. Finally, you will learn how and why Andrew Carnegie gave back to the people who helped him build his empire, and I will challenge you to do the same.

COMMISSION ONLY

As a business owner, it is always challenging to stress and worry about making payroll every two weeks, so one way to combat that is only to hire people on a pay-for-performance plan. If you are in a service-related business or in retail, this plan will be very difficult. However, if you own your own business as a one-person show . . . look and hire people who can sell for you on a commission-only basis, and in doing so, pay them through a commission pay plan.

As a result of implementing this kind of pay plan, you don't have to babysit your employees, track their hours, or worry about whether they are actually working or playing on company time. Also by operating this way, you only attract the most determined, disciplined, and serious business partners to help you move forward. Currently, I have upwards of 60 joint venture (JV) affiliate business partners who market my products and services, and when they make or refer sales, they get paid.

This topic reminds me of the very first salesperson who came to me asking for an opportunity. Believe it or not, as a professional speaker, people ask to assist me in my business virtually every time I speak in front of a large audience. As we will discuss in a later chapter, I am a big advocate of focusing on marketing my business—not on advertising it. Therefore, whenever I am out and about and run across a community bulletin board where business cards are tacked up, I always leave one there. I rarely get any business this way, but I figure, what the heck, it is only a one-penny business card.

Well, one day about five years after I launched my business, I posted a business card on a community bulletin board at a grocery store in Poulsbo, Washington. To my surprise, about five days later, I received a phone call from a very nice woman named Mary West. She was so impressed with my card that she invited me to attend her weekly networking meeting. I politely declined since I travel too much to commit to a weekly meeting. I figured I would just send her a free book and that would be the end of her. Well, she read my whole book in one day; then she went to my web site and noticed that anyone could purchase 100 copies of my book at half price, turn around and sell them at full price, and keep the profit. She then called me up and asked me when she could come by and drop off a $700 check and pick up the books. Hmm, I thought . . . perhaps I should reconsider joining her networking group.

To make a long story short, Mary has worked her way up in my organization and has booked tens of thousands of dollars in new business for me over the years, and I have promoted her to VP of Sales on a commission-only plan. As a result, she is free to work when she wants, as often as she wants, or as little as she wants. I recommend that you too offer the same kind of compensation plan and find very talented people like Mary West.

FINDING TALENT

Recently while visiting the East Coast for two speaking engagements, I extended my stay to catch one of my son's lacrosse games at Fairfield University. While on this same trip, I had the opportunity to stop in and speak to a group of seniors in an Entrepreneurship and Communications Business class at the University of Rhode Island in Kingston. The professor, Gail Lowney Alofsin (who happens to be a very inspirational and talented speaker in her own right) asked me to come in and speak to her class. She advised me that many of her students were worried about the next step in their lives once they graduated from college.

I accepted this opportunity to volunteer my time to help future entrepreneurs since I was passing through and already in the area for two other paid engagements. I spoke to the students for 90 minutes about taking an inventory of their top five passions, and then about going off and working a job for three to five years to gain the skill set, confidence, and connections needed prior to launching their own businesses. At the end of the speech, I held a Q&A session with them, and I was amazed by their willingness to ask questions.

The most memorable question was, "Mr. Snow, if you could give us just one bit of advice about how to transition to our next stage in life and create our own destinies, what would it be?" I chuckled and said, "I will give you my answer, but it needs to be a compound sentence." They all laughed. My answer was, "No matter what kinds of influences you have in your life trying to convince you to pursue a career other than the one you want, write a list of your top five passions and then spend the rest of your life pursuing those passions. And never, never, never give up on pursuing your dreams!"

My answer went over well, especially because I told them how I had succeeded by following my own passions in life. I could tell I had gotten the message through to these students because of their enthusiasm and willingness to ask questions and be inspired by what I had to say. Too often as a professional speaker, I wonder whether I am having an impact on people's lives because of how I can tell that they often perceive me. Many audience members just assume that a speaker is a multi, multimillionaire who doesn't understand real people and has not had to deal with the same real obstacles and adversities as everyone else. That is not at all the case, as I made clear to the students. You can succeed despite the problems you have, large and small. For example, as I write this chapter, my lawnmower is broken, and my grass is way too long. Also, the furnace in our home is malfunctioning and needs to be completely replaced. These are perfect examples of what we as speakers have to deal with on a daily basis—the same annoying little obstacles that all real people deal with each day as well as larger issues from health and family to income and car problems.

One day, not long after I spoke to the students at the University of Rhode Island, I was on a ferryboat heading into Seattle to give a speech. I stopped by the post office just before getting on the ferry to check my mail. To my surprise, I had received a package from Professor Gail Lowney Alofsin with a nice thank-you note sharing her appreciation for my having spoken to her class. But what was even more of a surprise was that included in this package were 21 letters from 21 of the attendees at the University of Rhode Island who had heard me speak. All of the attendees had written individual one- to two-page letters on their own letterheads expressing gratitude for my coming into their class to speak. Furthermore, each student told me how much of an impact my message had made on their lives, futures, and dreams. This package was such a surprise for me to receive and such a reinforcement and affirmation that I was on the right track. You can understand why I was so moved by their gratitude from a few of their comments I'll share with you now:

"I appreciated your advice that day that jobs can be beneficial to make "seed money" for your future."

—Eli

"It was very interesting that you have been laid off two times and here you are taking action to believe in what you can do for the world. Your formula to success is amazing to use as a life tool."

—Darnell

"I found your enthusiasm for life to be contagious. I left class that night feeling invigorated and ready to tackle all the projects that have been lingering in my head. You are right: why not start a business today?"

—David

"All my life I have wanted to produce music, but being such a risky business, I have never taken it too seriously. I think after your speech, I decided to stop trying to do what is safe and start doing what I am really passionate about, and I thank you for that."

—Rory

"After listening to you speak about the different courses you have taken throughout your life, I realized that I never want to be under someone else's authority. I want to be able to make it on my own, and you have opened the door to a new set of possibilities for me."

—Jill

My point in telling you this story is that $1 + 1$ does not equal 2 when it comes to performance and measuring results. Instead, $1 + 1$ may equal 3 or more. That is what masterminding is all about. I know the challenge you have is trying to build your business on your own. What I am suggesting you do is to go out and find a college student who wants to pursue a career in your industry and bring him or her on board to help you out. Some students might even be willing to volunteer 30, 60, or 90 days of their time to gain experience, add experience to their resumes, and learn the skill sets necessary to work toward eventually starting their own businesses. Perhaps you don't feel you can financially afford to add talent to help you. I would argue that you cannot afford not to bring on these additional resources. As I've already suggested, you can pay them on an incentive plan so that when they achieve or sell X dollars, they earn Y income.

I actually sent an e-mail to all of these students thanking them for their kind letters. I also offered all of them an opportunity to partner with me as JV Affiliates so they could actually make extra money while going to school. I would be surprised if those who replied back do not make some good extra money as affiliates, which they can use as seed money to fuel their passions.

For years, people have been talking about the importance of taking care of their customers, and obviously, I believe that is important. But management guru Joseph Juran points out that your internal customers are your employees, vendors, strategic partners, and anyone involved in the process of delivering the product or service to your external customer. I believe these internal customers are more important than the external customers.

EXERCISE

Therefore, I ask you to make a list of five people who are college students, or just graduating from college, who may have an interest in doing the type of work you do. Write out this list and then contact them to see whether any are interested in working with you to help you grow your business even more. If you don't know five college students, start asking friends, business associates, or contact your local university to find some.

1. _____

2. _____

3. _____

4. _____

5. _____

AFFLUENT ENTREPRENEUR PROFILE
ANDREW CARNEGIE

Andrew Carnegie was a businessman, industrialist, and entrepreneur who became a billionaire, mostly due to his success in the steel business prior to his dedication to philanthropy in his later years. He built the Carnegie Steel Company in Pittsburgh, Pennsylvania, which became responsible for much of the steel production throughout North America, and his product was used to build many of the early skyscrapers, railroads, and infrastructure on which the United States was built.

It was Carnegie's belief and philosophy that his job was not to mine the coal. He did not mold the steel manufactured in his plant into rails; he did not operate the furnaces. It was someone else who did these tasks. It was his employees who manufactured the steel. Therefore, his challenge was to find and hire the right people to do the right jobs to manufacture the steel for Carnegie Steel. He considered some of his proudest moments to be when he found those right people and saw the differences they were making. As a result, he believed that he had not created the wealth; the people, workers, and the nation were its creators. Consequently, he believed that he needed to give back this amassed wealth to those who made it in the first place. My point is twofold: Carnegie had to find and hire the right people, and then as the wealth was created, he was committed to giving it all back to them.

By the 1890s, Carnegie's enterprise had become one of the largest, most industrial enterprises in the modern world at the time. He built an estimated net worth of close to $300 billion in 2007 dollars. Then in his last 20 years of life, he dedicated himself to giving it all away,

(continued)

(*continued*)

back to the people who were responsible for creating it in the first place. He founded Carnegie Mellon University and ultimately gave away virtually all of his money to universities, schools, and libraries throughout North America and the United Kingdom.

EXERCISE

Who are the right people whom you can identify, hire, train, and delegate to help you build your empire? In the space below, write down the five key people already in your organization who will help you build your empire. Then beside each one's name, write in what you can do for that person to reward him or her for helping you to become an Affluent Entrepreneur.

1. _____
   _____
   _____

2. _____
   _____
   _____

3. _____
   _____
   _____

4. _____
   _____
   _____

5. _____
   _____
   _____

Summary

Finding and hiring the right people who believe in your vision to build your empire is one of the most difficult challenges you will face as an entrepreneur. If you can tackle this challenge, then you are destined for success. However, one of the biggest mistakes many entrepreneurs make is hiring people and promising them a salary. I firmly believe a salary is a recipe for disaster (at least during your business's early days).

One of my well-known speaking mentors has 47 employees on his payroll. He advises me that he has to speak virtually every day of the first three weeks of the month just to make overhead and payroll. Then, whatever engagements he does in the last week of the month he gets to keep as net profit for the company.

A better way exists. I firmly believe the better way is to pay on a performance basis, meaning that when your team members drive revenue to your company, they get paid. When they don't, you need not worry about babysitting or taking care of them. As a result of implementing a commission-only plan, you are going to attract only the best, brightest, and most determined business partners to help you achieve your revenue goals.

Where can you find the right people? Look around any and all college campuses, and you will find a multitude of talented, eager, and willing individuals to help you achieve your goals and visions. However, remember, just as Andrew Carnegie did, to do everything you can to take care of these internal customers; give back your wealth to those who made it, and you will not only achieve your financial goals as an entrepreneur, but you will also transcend your profit to give back to those in need, make a difference in this world, and leave your legacy.

Developing a "No Matter What" Mentality

> I will go anywhere, provided it is forward.
> —David Livingston

In this chapter you will learn how to develop a "No Matter What" mentality. This mantra has become a part of my DNA ever since hearing Les Brown speak on this subject back in 1990. As a business owner, you will face obstacles and adversity. But in that very situation is where you'll learn how to proceed and move forward even when you become a victim of Murphy's Law: "If anything can go wrong, it will." You will learn how to predetermine your future and never let rejection stop you in your tracks. You will learn what it takes to become *unstoppable* and to keep moving toward your vision, no matter what's happening around you. There's always a way, and in this chapter I will share with you how you too can develop a "No Matter What" mentality as you pursue any worthwhile dream or goal!

YOU DECIDE YOUR FUTURE

In my first book, *Creating Your Own Destiny*, I tried to convince my readers that ultimately, "If it is to be, it is up to me." That is often easier said than done. However, the longer I have studied successful people, the more I have realized that success leaves clues, and one clue that is more important than any other is the concept of "No Matter What."

I first learned this phrase while back in college from one of my all time favorite authors and speakers, Les Brown. Les has written several bestsellers, but two of my favorites are *Live Your Dreams* and *It's Not Over Until You Win*. In both of these books and in his live speeches, he teaches us that if we want success, then we need to develop a "No Matter What" mentality.

See, as a young child, Les's teachers labeled him as "Educably Mentally Retarded" (EMR). As a result of this label, he never worked hard in school; he never tried to excel in reading or writing; and for years, he fell behind in school. Finally, he was set free from that label one day when one of his teachers, Mr. Jackson, asked Les to come up and write something on the blackboard. Les responded that he was not able to do so because of his label.

In a moment, Mr. Jackson replied with a phrase that set Les free. He said, "Never let someone else's opinion of you become your reality." Les Brown applied that statement to the rest of his life and quickly developed a "No Matter What" mentality. Since then, he has become one of the most influential authors and speakers of our day.

WHERE THERE'S A WILL, THERE'S A WAY

After being so inspired by Les Brown, I knew deep down inside, even when a college senior, that I was going to become a professional speaker and best-selling author at some point in my life. I had no idea how I was going to do it, but I was determined to make it happen. That goal became the core of who I was and my biggest career goal to pursue. I was mocked by many people and rejected by dozens more, but I stayed true to my core beliefs and goals, which centered around the understanding that, "If it is to be, it is up to me." I asked myself the following set of questions (and still ask these questions today). I encourage you to ask the same questions of yourself as you develop your "No Matter What" mentality in terms of pursuing your goals and dreams:

If Not You, Then Who?

If Not This, Then What?

If Not Now, Then When?

I am convinced that these are the three most powerful questions in the English language. I persevered. At first, my former wife thought I was crazy. "My husband writing a book? Are you crazy? What qualifications do you have to attempt such lofty goals? What achievements in your life give you the belief system that says you can do this?" But those questions only made me focus on finding the answers and encouraged me all the more to do it. I answered all of her questions, convincing her and reconvincing myself I could do it, and then stayed firm to my mission.

To make a long story short, five years later, and $20,000 invested, I published *Creating Your Own Destiny* in 2001 at 140 pages with lots of grammar and spelling errors. I was so excited about the book that I quickly tried to hire a publicist. I sent this guy a check for $500, but he sent it back, telling me my book had no chance of being a success. He said I should give up on this project and keep my day job. Little did he know his rejection letter and returned check just added fuel to the fire.

By that point, Les Brown had already taught me never to let someone else's opinion of me determine my reality. As a result of this rejection, I was more determined than ever to prove this skeptic wrong. Ten editions later, now in hard cover, roughly 300 pages, and published by John Wiley & Sons, Inc., I am happy to say that my first book has sold over 150,000 copies in five languages in 108 countries. While it is by no means at the Harry Potter level of sales, it has done multiple times better than 99 percent of books that, according to Dan Poynter in *The Self-Publishing Manual*, sell an average of 600 to 700 copies.

THERE IS ALWAYS A WAY

You are going to face some big problems in pursuit of becoming a successful business owner and eventually an Affluent Entrepreneur. But I'm going to provide you some firsthand answers to these problems since I have encountered many of the same obstacles along the way. My solutions focus upon how, as an Affluent Entrepreneur, you must think and act if you are to achieve what the subtitle of this book promises: Prosperity.

Problem: I need a bank loan to be able to run or expand my business.
Solution: Make more sales, and use revenue to support growth of business.

Problem: I am not getting along with my business partner.
Solution: Get rid of the business partner, and keep 100 percent control of the business.

Problem: The economy is causing my poor sales.
Solution: Develop new markets to sell to, and prospect extra hard to drive more revenue.

Problem: My credit score is dinged, and I can't finance growth.
Solution: Either pay cash for all business expansion, or use other people's money (OPM).

Problem: There is not enough time in the day to get everything done that I need to do.
Solution: Delegate work to virtual assistants to free you up for your most important duties.

Problem: My spouse is not supporting me emotionally in this venture.
Solution: Prove your spouse is wrong by collecting a big check, and buying him or her something special.

Problem: I can't afford the needed office space to grow my business.
Solution: Work from home virtually, and have all others in your business do the same.

Problem: My car is broken down, and I can't afford another.
Solution: Walk, bike, or use public transportation.

Problem: I am not good at marketing, selling, and prospecting.
Solution: Get good at it, or hire someone on commission-only to perform these duties.

Problem: The economy is bad right now, and no one is buying.
Solution: Refuse to participate in a recession.

Bottom line, whatever obstacle, roadblock, or adversity you are facing, there is *always* a "No Matter What" solution. Every entrepreneur before you has encountered the same challenges you have. Those who refused to quit or give up always succeeded. Let's face it; the only way an entrepreneur can fail is to stop, quit, and give up. Les Brown has always said, "If you can look up, you can get up!"

I believe the temporary setbacks are part of the equation. In fact, I believe a major financial setback is a setup for a comeback. And everyone loves to watch the underdog come back and win the game. With each setback you experience in life, you become a stronger, more experienced navigator. Never give in, never give up, never lose hope, and you will make it!

EXERCISE A

List all the road blocks, obstacles, and challenges that you face in your life as a struggling entrepreneur. Now list your biggest five challenges below:

1. _____
   _____
   _____

2. _____
   _____
   _____

3. _____
   _____
   _____

4. _____
   _____
   _____

5. _____
   _____
   _____

EXERCISE B

Thinking like an Affluent Entrepreneur by putting to use your "No Matter What" mentality, write in your own solution below to every problem listed in the above exercise:

1. _____
   _____
   _____

2. _____
   _____
   _____

3. _____
   _____
   _____

4. _____
   _____
   _____

5. _____
   _____
   _____

AFFLUENT ENTREPRENEUR PROFILE
MARTHA STEWART

In 1981 at 40 years of age, Martha Stewart owned a very successful catering business in Westport, Connecticut. However, she soon realized that if she just continued down this path, her grandchildren would never really know what she stood for other than that she was good at entertaining and hosting parties. Therefore, her vision was to write a book. Not just any kind of book, but the quintessential book about the art of entertaining. This "Kitchen Goddess" soon published her first book *Entertaining*, and not long thereafter, she followed it up with a string of seven additional books. All were huge hits.

Next came her magazine *Martha Stewart Living*, her web site, her mail-order business, TV show, and the launch of her Kmart line. Eventually, her empire was built, and Martha Stewart Living Omnimedia went public in October of 1999. Just as her company experienced unparalleled growth, it all seemed to plummet as a result of her serving a five-month term in a federal correctional facility for misleading investigators about a stock sale she made with insider information that had not yet gone public.

This setback may have done in most entrepreneurs, but not Martha Stewart. She took this adversity head on, developed a "No Matter What" mentality, regained composure, and started back up right where she had left off.

At first Stewart's stock value tanked, but through her hard work, dedication, and unwavering commitment to rebound, her magazine gained more ad sales, her NBC talk show became a hit, and today, she continues to

(continued)

(continued)

launch new products. She now has food products at Costco, a wine label, and housewares at Macy's. Yes indeed, Martha Stewart is back and she is unstoppable. For her tireless work ethic, Martha Stewart has amassed a net worth of $638 million.[1]

SUMMARY

No Matter What! Those are the three most important words in the Affluent Entrepreneur's language. As you begin to gain control of your self-talk, let your heart become a driving force and your vision become the ultimate goal; then, you will know there is always a way to get from here to there; we just need to pursue every angle.

Whether it is Martha Stewart's legal challenges or your own specific roadblock, Affluent Entrepreneurs always succeed if they are never willing to give up, give in, or stop fighting. Sometimes when you feel everything is against you, you need to reach down inside you, gather up your intestinal fortitude and every ounce of strength, every bit of fight inside of you, and unleash this rage creatively (without doing harm to anyone or anything), and fight like hell to protect unseen circumstances from stealing your dreams.

Remember, when life has you down, never, ever give up! If you get knocked down seven times, get up eight. Know that whether or not you think you have the strength to make it, be assured that the power is deep inside you, waiting patiently to pull you through. If you don't already know it, Google and read Mary Stevenson's famous poem "Footprints in the Sand" and you'll understand what I mean. Just know that if your vision and dreams are for the greater good of humanity, your solution will be realized!

---

[1] According to Wikipedia, but in 2005, according to Forbes Annual list she was a billionaire, http://money.cnn.com/2005/03/10/news/newsmakers/forbes_billionaires/index.htm

Participating in a Mastermind Group

Ambition leads me not only farther than any other man has been before me, but as far as I think it is possible for man to go.

—James Cook

In this chapter, you will learn why participating in a mastermind group is like pushing the accelerator pedal and steering your way toward success. I will introduce you to what a mastermind group is, what it is not, and how to select group members who will help you to benefit the best from other people's knowledge, experience, and networks. You will also learn how to conduct your own mastermind group meetings. Finally, you will learn from Harvey Firestone and Henry Ford, and you will become inspired to incorporate a whole new way of earning revenues for your company without having to borrow money from Angel Investors.

MASTERMIND DEFINED

In his must-read classic *Think and Grow Rich*, Napoleon Hill described a mastermind group in this way: "The coordination of knowledge and effort of two or more people, who work toward a definite purpose, in the spirit of harmony. No two minds ever come together without thereby creating a third, invisible and intangible force, which may be likened to a third mind (the master mind)."[1]

---

[1] http://www.sacred-texts.com/nth/tgr/tgr15.htm

Mastermind groups can come in many different shapes and forms. Some are big; some are small. Some last a long time, while others go by the wayside. Twice, I have joined other people's mastermind groups and have benefited on both occasions. Additionally, I have created my own publishing/speaking mastermind group and have members from all over the world who participate weekly by way of a phone conference call. All of us support each other in our writing and speaking pursuits.

One of the coolest things I like about masterminding is the amount of quality time you get to spend with other entrepreneurs and how you get to soak up their knowledge as a result. One of the challenges a small business owner has is that often you will spend so much time building your business that you don't really get enough time, or any time, to hang with your buddies to compare notes, bounce ideas back and forth, and benefit from other people's business skills and unique talents.

For example, today I just spent two hours with my buddy and mastermind partner Denny Andrews, who is the founder and owner of Denny Andrews Consulting (www.DennyAndrews Consulting.com). Denny works with businesses of all sizes on their online presence, and he bills out at $400–500 per hour helping entrepreneurs leverage technology to maximize online visibility. He set me up with three different Facebook ads, and he showed me how, for just a few hundred dollars per month, my tiny ad would market my book and speaking business to upward of 2 million Facebook members who specifically enjoy reading and entrepreneurship. It took Denny hundreds of hours to master his marketing skills and acquire his wisdom, but because we are buddies and part of the same mastermind group, he did it for me as a favor. If I hadn't known him, it would have cost me $1,500 or more.

What a Mastermind Group Is

1. Like-minded individuals getting together to help the other group members succeed.

2. Accountability partners to help each other achieve short- and long-term goals.

3. Weekly, biweekly, monthly meetings to assess progress.

4. Strategic sessions with one leader giving homework to each member and debriefing.

5. A small group of 5–12 members.

6. Typically, no two members are in competing businesses.

7. An opportunity to share in complete confidence.

8. Brainstorming sessions to share expertise.

What a Mastermind Group Is Not

1. Social hour just to visit and tell stories.

2. Something that is optional to attend.

3. A coaching, networking atmosphere.

4. A leads group.

5. A group where you are continuously bringing in new members.

6. Dominated by one speaker telling all how to run their businesses.

7. Mixed with both employees and business owners.

8. Paid membership.

MEETING AGENDA

Typically, each meeting should last between one and two hours, depending on how many people are present. If your group is 4–6 people you can probably get through the meeting in 60 minutes. If you have 10–12 attendees, I think you are better off having the meeting last two hours.

Ideally, you should try to meet a minimum of once per month. Anything less than that will lose momentum quickly. I don't encourage weekly meetings because that is just too often, and your group is bound to fall apart. Every other week or once per month is ideal.

Meetings should start with one person serving as the chair or floor person. That person then asks the others to debrief and share their successes and failures since their last meeting. The chairperson should keep track of time to make certain no one dominates the conversation and that all get adequate time to check in, so to speak. This check-in should last approximately one-third of the allocated time for which the meeting is to occur.

The middle one-third of the meeting can be a variety of things. It can be one of the members having her business showcased in front of the others while asking for feedback, advice, or strategy from the others in the mastermind group. It can be a debriefing from a movie the group has watched, a book the group has read, or a speech or seminar the group has attended. It is this portion of the meeting where ideas and brainstorming are meant to flow freely in such a way that all attendees may gather ideas to implement in their business in the weeks to come. In the past, my mastermind group has even watched videos from an online e-learning company such as iLearningGlobal's Daily Success Stream (www.DailySuccessStream.com). Based on the content of the video, we will brainstorm how we can apply what we just watched to our businesses.

Finally, the last one-third of the meeting will again be run by the chair who will encourage everyone in the group to go around the room and publicly announce to the group the goals they absolutely will commit to achieving prior to the next meeting. These publicly stated goals will become your top priority to achieve in the time between meetings. Often, I recommend at this point that you get one of the others in the group to become your accountability partner so you can call each other prior to the next meeting to check in, and you can encourage each other to follow through and actually achieve all the goals publicly announced in the previous meeting.

More than just meeting together, often these mastermind partners will become your best friends. You will most likely hang out with them more than your other friends, may go to ball games together, or even on vacation. Often, mastermind members will hold competitions with each other, such as to achieve certain levels of weight loss by a certain date and time, or by placing different types of wagers here or there. Most importantly, everything that is discussed in these mastermind groups is kept 100 percent confidential to anyone outside the group.

WHO SHOULD BE YOUR MASTERMIND PARTNERS?

There is an old saying that you are the sum of the five people you hang out with the most. If you hang out with unemployed, homeless drug dealers, chances are good you will end up an unemployed, homeless drug dealer.

Conversely, if you hang around millionaires and billionaires, then sooner or later through the power of association and the Law of Attraction, you too will eventually become a millionaire or billionaire. My point is that you need to be very careful about whom you select to join your mastermind group. Be aware and steer clear of negative people, toxic people, and pessimists. Also stay away from lifelong career employee types who still believe it is possible to make it in the long term by being employed for a company.

You want risk takers in your group: People who already own and operate their own businesses or who are slowly making the transition to doing so. You want positive, optimistic, supportive, free enterprise capitalists with monster goals. These are the kinds of people you want in your group. People who believe it is not the government's role to overmanage and provide handouts for all, but rather the government's role to lead, and to allow small business owners the freedom to do what they do best, which is to create products and services to solve problems in the marketplace.

Finally, you have a couple of options here. You can decide purposely to find these contacts and connections of yours from among people all in the same industry so that everyone better understands each other's business. Or you can decide that perhaps it makes more sense intentionally to put your group together with members who are each from different industries so you do not compete with one another.

EXERCISE

Take an inventory of all of your closest friends in your network. Now ask yourself of these friends and contacts, who are the ones you believe best meet the descriptions above. Once you have these people in mind, go ahead and write down 10 of their names in the area below. Invite 10 to join and know that maybe only 6 will be able to commit to participating for the long haul.

1. _____

2. _____

3. _____

4. _____

5. _____

6. _____

7. _____

8. _____

9. _____

10. _____

AFFLUENT ENTREPRENEUR PROFILE
HENRY FORD

Henry Ford became a very talented inventor as a young man. One thing led to another until soon he was building one of the first gasoline-powered automobiles. He eventually founded Ford Motor Company on June 16, 1903, after working as a Chief Engineer for Thomas Edison's Edison Illuminations Company in his younger years. It was there he was introduced to Thomas Edison.

This relationship with Edison and later his friendship with Harvey Firestone, founder of Firestone Tire and Rubber Company, allowed the three of them to create a very unique gathering of the minds, which they named "The Millionaires' Club." They lived up to the name— Ford, Edison, and Firestone were considered the three most influential leaders of their time in American business. As a result, they would often purchase buildings or other items for one another without any formal agreements or handshakes, just each other's word.

It was during these meetings, vacations, and time they spent together that Ford shared his dilemma about what should be Ford Motor Company's vision. While there is some debate as to who created the first mass assembly line and where it was located, it is commonly agreed that Henry Ford is the one who achieved this feat in American business history. When Ford shared his cash flow concern in relation to how to mass-produce his automobiles with his two friends, Firestone suggested he presell his vehicles and use the money from those presales to fund the first mass assembly line.

Ford did exactly what his mastermind partner, Firestone, suggested. He presold an estimated 375,000

(continued)

(*continued*)

automobiles at roughly $600 per vehicle and raised approximately $225 million in revenues for the company. These monies were used to build the assembly lines that would mass-produce the presold automobiles. As a result, Ford Motor Company became one of the biggest manufacturers of automobiles throughout the world, having a dealership in every midsized city in the United States and in all the major cities throughout the world. When Henry Ford died in 1947, according to *Forbes Magazine* he had amassed a fortune of almost $190 billion in 2008.

EXERCISE

After I inform my publishing clients about this presales model, I often suggest they follow it to presell their books in advance. One of my clients, Michael Price, sold close to $2,500 worth of his book titled *Fearless Thinking* prior to its even hitting the press. He used these funds to cover his printing bill. Therefore, think for a moment of products or services you create as an entrepreneur and write below three of them that you can market using this presales model.

1. _____

   _____

   _____

2. _____

   _____

   _____

3. _____

   _____

   _____

Summary

I firmly believe that if you are serious about becoming an Affluent Entrepreneur, you must either join a mastermind group or go out and start your own. I know what you may be thinking: *How in the world can I squeeze this into my already busy schedule?* My response is, "How can you afford not to benefit from all the proven strategies, techniques, and ideas that this 'third mind' can and will offer your business?"

I challenge you to stop whatever you are doing and make it a priority to identify the right kinds of people for your group. Then begin your group in earnest. I promise you that within the first six months, as a result of applying the collective wisdom from your group, you will experience measurable results in terms of increased revenues to your bottom line.

Moving forward, always think of the presales model implemented by Henry Ford as a result of Harvey Firestone's suggestion in The Millionaires Club, and see how you can do the same within your business. In doing so, you will be less dependent on bank loans, other people's money (OPM), and angel investors, and better equipped to provide solutions to your customers' problems.

Finally, I challenge you to reread and study Napoleon Hill's books including *Think and Grow Rich* and *The Law of Success*. In doing so, it will accelerate your personal development as the CEO of your company while reducing the amount of time it will take you to become an Affluent Entrepreneur.

Outsourcing Your Non–Revenue-Producing Tasks

Unless a man undertakes more than he can possibly do, he will never do all that he can.
—Henry Drummond

I n this chapter, you will learn why it's important to hire a book-keeper to pay your bills and any and all other non–revenue-producing tasks that are impacting your prospecting and sales results. You'll also learn why it's important to use virtual assistants and others so you can focus most of your energies on what you do best—driving revenues to your company. You will learn about creating a Virtual Board of Directors and how to embrace change for the betterment of your company. Finally, you will learn how and why Sam Walton of Wal-Mart successfully navigated these same issues to change retailing forever.

BOOKKEEPER

According to Sandy Botkin, attorney, CPA, and former IRS legal specialist, there are two reasons why most Americans never achieve wealth. First, they fail to save 10 percent of their income. Second, they overpay their taxes year after year. As an entrepreneur, you must retain the services of a skilled accountant who understands and applies the existing laws as they apply to the business owner, and here you'll learn how to make the best decision in finding one.

Have you ever been frustrated with your own personal finances? So much so that as your business grows and your family grows, you literally seem to have a bill due virtually every day of the month? Well, you are not alone. I too have struggled with these issues for years and years. During my darkest financial days, I would spend 2–3 hours per day just dealing with paying bills, allocating my budget, and taking calls from collectors.

After a while, it got so bad and out of control, with too many bills and too many due dates that I could not stay on top of it any longer. During my darkest days financially, I figured that I no longer needed to worry about when the bills were due because when they were due, the creditors would just call me, and I would make all my payments over the phone, eliminating the need to write out and mail checks. Well as you can imagine, that was not a very good solution since too many times my cell phone would be shut off, or I would pay way too much in late fees, not to mention I was getting my credit dinged. What I finally realized was that I simply hate accounting, paying bills, and anything to do with money leaving my bank account. I love adding money to my account, but I dislike it going out.

Finally, I tracked down one of the most successful entrepreneurs in my community. This woman was the most successful real estate agent on Bainbridge Island. When I asked her to share with me her secret, she replied, "Do what you are good at and hire others to do what you are not good at."

This solution seemed obvious to me, so when she said the best decision she ever made was to hire a personal bookkeeper to pay all of her bills (both business and personal), I decided it was time to do the same.

Fortunately, I just happened to know her bookkeeper because of my involvement with the board of directors for our high school lacrosse team. Her name is Nancy, and she has become a godsend to my business. I meet with her every two weeks for 60–90 minutes each time; she tells me which bills we should pay, and I put in my two cents' worth; then she goes online and pays all my bills, both personal and business.

As a result, I have not paid a single bill in at least four years. No mortgage payments, car payments, power bills, cell bills, insurance, none, zip, zero. As a result, I have taken the 60–90 minutes per day that I used to spend dealing with finances, and now I apply it elsewhere, by prospecting for speaking engagements or being creative with my time and working on writing books or marketing my business. Without question, hiring a bookkeeper has been the single greatest enhancement to my business and has allowed me to pursue the Affluent Entrepreneur lifestyle.

EXERCISE

In the space provided below, write in the name of your personal bookkeeper. If you don't have this person yet working for you, write in the name here once you have hired that person.

Next, so you don't drag out this search for 18 months, write in the date you will have this person working on your team.

VIRTUAL ASSISTANTS

I first started using virtual assistants (VAs) several years ago after I read Timothy Ferriss's book *The 4-Hour Work Week*. What I learned was that there are things in my business I like to do and am good at that drive revenue to my bottom line. Conversely, some things I am not good at, don't like to do, and they also steal precious prospecting time from my business.

In his book, Ferriss shares his ideas on how to have much of your work done for you by other people. The reason why this principle is so powerful is you have to determine your true value as an entrepreneur. And if you want to become an Affluent Entrepreneur, you need to be even more careful and more selective about how you spend your time. If your hourly billing rate is $250, for example, then any task you currently perform that you can find someone else to do better, at a rate less than $250 per hour, you should outsource so you can free up your time to do more of what you are good at.

There are two enemies that you as the Affluent Entrepreneur need to be aware of: (1) e-mail and (2) other administrative/busy work that produces no revenue for your company. What I mean is, it is better for your desk and office to be a mess while you are bringing in a huge amount of revenue, than to have the cleanest, sparkling office in the world and the most organized e-mail inbox with little or no incoming revenue.

If you think you can outsource or contract the sales, marketing, and prospecting piece of your business, think again. You want your VAs to be doing the admin work, the e-mail work, the return calls, while you focus exclusively on the activities that drive revenue to your company's bottom line.

Most Affluent Entrepreneurs are good at prospecting, selling, and marketing. So if that is the case with you, my argument is that you should spend your time performing these duties and let all the other required work be left to someone more qualified whom you can contract to do this work for you at a lesser price.

EXERCISE

List the 10 biggest roles you play in your company. What are the 10 most important things you do to keep your company afloat, drive revenue, and see that all the "t's" are crossed and the "i's" are dotted. Once these duties are listed below, circle the ones you actually really enjoy. Whatever roles are left uncircled are the roles you need to delegate to other people, whether they are employees, or contract/virtual assistants.

1. _____

2. _____

3. _____

4. _____

5. _____

6. _____

7. _____

8. _____

9. _____

10. _____

In my business as an author, speaker, and coach, I delegate out the following roles to other people, none of whom are employees of my business, but all are business partners, suppliers, or vendors:

- Bookkeeper (pays all my bills)

- VP of Sales (assists me in my prospecting pursuits)

- Accountant (keeps me on the up and up with the IRS)

- Web Master (handles every detail of my web site and keeps it updated)

- Editor/Proofreader (checks and edits all my written correspondence)

- IT Expert (keeps my computer running smoothly)

- JV Partners (continuously bring referrals to the table to close)

- And so on . . .

VIRTUAL BOARD OF DIRECTORS

In business, you need people to turn to, people who have been there and done that. Ideally, it is great if you can find those people in your mastermind group, but that may not be the case if they are in different industries. Additionally, many of your mastermind attendees may be local, and you need someone else's perspective from a different point of view.

So I encourage you to create a Virtual Board of Directors. These people are advisors you know, like, and trust, who feel the same way about you. Perhaps a former college professor, a former sales manager, a classmate, or even a successful relative would make a good advisor or person whom you can bounce ideas off. My point is this: Use their talents, skill sets, wisdom, and advice for your company's benefit. Perhaps it may be unrealistic to contact all of them every month, but make it a point that no matter what, you have a one-hour phone call monthly with at least one of these Virtual Board of Directors members. These board members don't even really need to know of the others involved or of the board itself. It is okay if they think you just want to gather advice from them every now and again.

EXERCISE

In the space below, write in the five most qualified, most trusted, and most successful Virtual Board of Directors members you would like to add to your team.

1. _____
2. _____
3. _____
4. _____
5. _____

AFFLUENT ENTREPRENEUR PROFILE
SAM WALTON

Sam Walton got his start in retailing back in 1945 after he got out of the army. He borrowed $20,000 from his father-in-law and added that to $5,000 of his own money he had saved to purchase a Ben Franklin variety store in Newport, Arkansas. Walton's philosophy from the start was to treat employees with the respect they deserved, including through profit sharing and decision making. As a result, all his employees were called "associates."

Walton's experience at this first store would forever change the way the retail distribution business would operate in the future. By buying wholesale goods in bulk from the lowest-price supplier, Walton was able to pass the savings on to his customers who in turn generated more sales. Additionally, Sam Walton pioneered the concept of extended hours during the Christmas holiday season. This new way of doing business was so successful that Walton went on to open numerous other Ben Franklin stores and Walton's Five and Dime stores. The first actual Wal-Mart opened in 1962 in Rogers, Arizona.

Today Wal-Mart is proud of it roots and operates 4,269 stores in 14 countries including the United States, employing 1.5 million "associates." Each week Wal-Mart has 138 million customers shopping in its stores throughout the world. Because of the tremendous changes Sam Walton brought to retailing, before he passed away in 1992, he had amassed a net worth of $25 billion, equal to nearly $40 billion in 2010.

SUMMARY

Just as Sam Walton pioneered an industry and changed the way retailing was done, you need to change your business model. You can't do everything. You need to get out of your own way. Delegate what you can to your employees, and what they cannot do, outsource to other contract workers, suppliers, or vendors who can perform the job at hand more efficiently than you.

When you learn to let go and trust others to earn their stripes so to speak, it will free up your schedule to perform the absolutely most important role you have as the CEO of your own company. That role is to drive revenue to your bottom line. Without revenue, your company will perish. With revenue, all things are possible.

As you get better and better at making these changes and empowering others on your team, you will set yourself up to pioneer your industry and to become a true Affluent Entrepreneur!

Securing Win-Win Transactions

Your best teacher is your last mistake.
—Ralph Nader

S uccessful entrepreneurs understand the needs of their current and potential customers. In this chapter, I will offer you several strategies to help you identify and understand your customers' goals, needs, and desires. You'll learn to appreciate what your customers are looking for in life and how you can help meet their needs. As a result, you can and will offer win-win transactions to your customers, which in turn will build your business and drive revenue to your company's bottom line. You'll then have the satisfaction of having your business thrive and knowing you've truly helped someone. In this chapter, you will also learn how billionaire Richard Branson conducted a huge win-win transaction to help turn the economy around with his purchase of 18 commercial planes.

GOING THE EXTRA MILE

Win-win transactions are a must if you are to market your products and services successfully and become an Affluent Entrepreneur. A perfect example of a win-win transaction is an opportunity I recently had to speak for the Subway Restaurant world conference in Chicago in the summer of 2010. My vice president of sales discovered the contact information for Subway's meeting planner on the Internet. It turned out the meeting planner was in

Connecticut, and it just so happened that I was scheduled for a speaking engagement in New England and would also be visiting my son, who attended Fairfield University.

I immediately sent out a signed copy of my book and my speaker kit. I then followed that up with an e-mail advising the meeting planner that I was going to be in town, and I would ideally like to drop by for a visit/interview. She agreed, and we set a date to meet. When I visited her, we hit it off well, but I had one more curve ball to throw her (and little did I know she was going to blast it out of the park).

As we departed, I said, "There is one more thing. If you are going to consider me as one of your speakers for your Chicago conference, then I am offering to volunteer a half day of my life to go into a Subway Restaurant and work alongside your other workers. I'm willing to bake bread, make cookies, fix sandwiches, even take out the trash." She looked at me with shock and said, "Why in the world would you offer to do that?" I replied, "Doing so is the only way I can learn firsthand the challenges, issues, and obstacles that Subway franchise owners face on a daily basis. With this information, I will be able to customize and create a presentation specifically geared to address that challenge."

I will never forget the expression on her face. She told me she had been booking speakers for 20-plus years, and not once had a speaker ever offered to volunteer to work in a restaurant in preparation for his speech. I walked out the door feeling very good about this meeting. On a later speaking trip to New England, I stopped by again in person while passing through and dropped off the updated John Wiley & Sons, Inc. edition of my book *Creating Your Own Destiny*. As a result, a few weeks later, she e-mailed me to let me know I was selected as one of their speakers.

And by the way, she did take me up on my offer to work in a Subway Restaurant. I never worked so hard in my entire life. During the lunch hours, the line of customers never seemed to end. I learned about the Subway terms of food rationing and "through-put." I learned that I wanted to eat the product while I was working because it smelled so good. My favorite part of the day was when the big guy came through the line and demanded, "Don't skimp on the tuna!"

Having the opportunity to walk a mile in the owner's shoes, to be behind the counter, and to get to appreciate the employees' daily tasks, made all the difference in the world in my understanding of my customer's perspective, challenges, issues, pains, and fears. It also taught me how to make a great sub. Now ask yourself this question: "How well do I empathize with and know my customers?"

Without question, the above situation is a perfect example of creating a win-win situation and get more speaking engagements. This experience allowed me to create a more customized and humorous presentation. Better yet, I learned this idea from one of my publishing clients, John DiPietro, who is a member of my Inner Circle Publishing Mastermind group; John is the author of *You Don't Have to Be Perfect to Be Great*. John used to sell radio advertising to McDonald's, and he and his team would also use this volunteer strategy; he advised me that it always worked. By leveraging his knowledge, I had ensured my chance for a win-win situation.

EXERCISE

List five ways you can change your approach so you can offer win-win solutions to your clients and go the extra mile:

1. _____

2. _____

3. _____

4. _____

5. _____

ABOVE AND BEYOND

One of my mentors, as a professional speaker, once told me that it doesn't really matter what you say on the platform during your speech (assuming you do a good job entertaining the audience). What matters is your interaction with your audience and with the meeting planner before and after your speech.

Over the years after having given more than 1,500 speaking engagements, I have come to realize the truth of this. Therefore, I do everything I can when I speak to show up early to network with the audience or even, as is often the case, to have breakfast with them. Next, I try to go around the table, meet everyone, and shake hands. Ideally, I also want to pick out a few of them to interview so I can learn what their challenges and issues are with their current position.

Part of my unique offering as a professional speaker is always to conduct a one-hour prespeech interview with the meeting planner; as a result, I can learn the following about their organization: what is working, what is not, and, most important, what are their goals for the conference.

With this information, I will typically customize the entire middle portion of my speech specifically to address those goals. I have come to realize that many speakers do not customize their speeches to their audience's needs, and this failure to be relevant always comes back to hurt them later with negative ratings on their evaluation forms. It can also lead to not being invited back for future speaking engagements, and a failure to achieve the important word of mouth that leads to being referred to engagements for other groups.

With this foundation laid, I want to tell a true story that occurred recently during a speech I gave in Nashua, New Hampshire. After having already been on the road for three days, I was tired and just wanted to check into my hotel and go to bed. Earlier in the week, I had flown out of Seattle on a red-eye flight to Boston so that I could drive to Connecticut that day to watch my son play in a college lacrosse game. I spent the night in Connecticut, and the next day I drove to the University of Rhode Island where I gave a speech to the school's Entrepreneurship class. I spent that night in Newport, Rhode Island, but only after I attended a networking event where I met several meeting planners. The following day, I woke up and drove to Providence, Rhode Island, where I delivered yet another speech to a hospitality group. Next, I drove to Boston and hung out with my best friend since third grade, Dave Beauchamp. We visited for a couple of hours before I went to Winchester, Massachusetts, to have a fantastic dinner with my aunt, uncle, and cousins. After dinner, I had still not checked into my hotel in Nashua, where I was to deliver a speech the next morning.

I finally left my cousin's house around 8:30 PM and got to my hotel room and checked in around 9:30 PM. I was exhausted, having been on the road for 3–4 days. During that time, my e-mail had been screwed up, and as a result, I was way, way behind on reading e-mails—perhaps as many as 300–400 of them were yet unread.

So there I sat in my hotel room, exhausted, desperately wanting just to go to bed and crash. However, it has always been my policy as a professional speaker to call the meeting planner upon arrival so it is known I am there. This courtesy is especially important when you are the opening keynote speaker the next morning, since you don't want the meeting planner to stay up all night tossing and turning from worrying about whether or not the keynote speaker's plane has landed or not. You want to give the meeting planner as much peace of mind as possible. Think about it: There are a million things that could go wrong for a conference, and the meeting planner is already stressed about putting on a world-class event, so the last thing he or she needs to worry about is travel delays with the keynote speaker.

Therefore, once I got into my room, I threw down my bags, plugged in my cell phone and laptop to charge them, and then called the meeting planner to advise him that I had arrived. He was thrilled to hear from me, gave me his suite number, and told me that several others who were part of the planning committee were in a suite down the hall, and he invited me to come down for a beer to say hello. Well, since I don't drink, I politely declined his offer for a beer as I always do, but certainly, given my philosophy of going above and beyond, I went down to meet the planning committee members, even though it was now 10 PM, and I just desperately wanted to crash.

When I reached the room, I was amazed by what I saw upon entering. There were five or six other meeting planners in the room, and they were busy stuffing conference registration folders with schedules, brochures, photos, name badges, and several other inserts. I could tell they were desperate to get this done since each of the piles yet to be inserted was over six inches high.

I thought to myself, "I could be polite and visit for a few moments and then go back to bed, or I can do what my mentor taught me—arrive early and stay late." You guessed it—against every bit of common sense I had in my body, I rolled up my sleeves, pulled up a comfortable chair, and sat down with the rest of them to start stuffing registration packets. Through this process, I rubbed my fingertips raw and got even more tired, but as a team, we finally finished putting the registration packets together just before midnight.

The others were blown away that they had just spent 90 minutes with the keynote speaker and, more important, that he was willing to roll up his sleeves and help them stuff the registration packets. My mentor would have been proud of me for helping out that evening. The next morning, my keynote speech went off without a hitch, and now everyone there was even more eager to refer me to other organizations for additional future speaking engagements. Without question, I firmly believe this kind of experience is a win-win transaction. The meeting planners get to spend more time with the speaker, and the speaker ends up with more referrals as a result.

EXERCISE

As an Affluent Entrepreneur, what are five strategies, techniques, or ideas you can implement into your business to go above and beyond to create a win-win situation for your clients?

1. _____

   _____

   _____

2. _____

   _____

   _____

3. _____

   _____

   _____

4. _____

   _____

   _____

5. _____

   _____

   _____

LOOK TO IMPLEMENT A WIN-WIN WITH YOUR FAMILY

Win-win should not just be applied to your clients, but also to your family. I suspect that in the process of building your business, your family has given up many things and made sacrifices along the way. Well, if your family is like mine that is certainly the case.

Several years ago, maybe when I was 23 years old, a co-worker I admired gave me some tremendous financial advice that has served me well over the years. She said that when buying cars, purchase the most affordable used car that you like and want to drive since cars depreciate over time. Conversely she said, buy the most expensive, nicest house you can afford to buy (even if you have to eat macaroni, hot dogs, and beans) since houses almost always appreciate in value over time.

For the most part, I have taken this advice except on two occasions. I have purchased brand-new cars on two occasions, and in both cases, I have realized I probably could have gotten an almost equally good used car and saved a whole lot of money. Let's face it, after you drive your new car for a month, it is no longer a "new car" but a "used car."

Long story short, back in 2000, I was rolling in money. I was making well over six figures in high-tech corporate sales selling printed circuit boards. At this time, I was still very much building my speaking business on a part-time basis, but I was full-time in my sales career and could see no end in sight for it as my income continued to increase. Meanwhile, the car I was driving was a high-mileage, former company car from my previous sales job. It was starting to break down and needed some costly repairs.

My family and I talked about it and decided we wanted a new car; we had fallen in love with the Saab brand; so we did our due diligence and a few weeks later found ourselves in Seattle at a Saab dealership. As soon as we walked into the dealership, my former wife pointed to a red Saab 9-3 convertible, smiled, and said, "Now this is what I am talking about." But since we had two young boys and lived in Seattle where it rains five months out of the year, we both agreed that a convertible wasn't practical at that point in our lives.

In the end, we found ourselves attracted to the Saab 9-5 sedan with a large enough backseat for our two boys. We fell in love with the car, and we hand-selected the exact one we wanted. It was a blue Saab 9-5, 2000 model, with sunroof, beige leather seats (both with air-conditioned and heated seats). It was sleek, sharp, fast, and, oh yes, even turbo.

Since we had high incomes and perfect credit, we easily qualified to purchase this $40,000 vehicle. However, the purchase would have caused us to have an $800 per month payment, so we instead went with the lease option, which meant turning in our existing car to serve as the down payment. By going with the lease, our payment was $500 instead of $800, which we felt was the better option.

Over the next five years, we put 65,000 miles on the car and absolutely fell in love with it. It serviced our needs perfectly. It was stylish, roomy, fast, and it soon became my former wife's favorite car, while I was often stuck driving our Suburban. During those five years we drove the Saab, everything seemed to fall apart for us financially. If you've read my previous book, *Creating Your Own Destiny*, you will have learned that at 9/11, I was laid off, and then laid off again in 2002. As a consequence, I prematurely attempted to go full time with my speaking business without having enough opportunities in my sales funnel. I ended up getting behind on our bills, liquidated our savings to invest in my business, and also saw our perfect credit score get substantially dinged. When 2005 came, it was time to turn in our Saab, but we both loved it too much just to let it go. We investigated purchasing the vehicle, which was now valued at about $20,000, but due to our credit score we were unable to get a loan for that amount.

Therefore, I had to turn it into the dealership since our lease was up. As a result, we purchased a 20-year-old beater that was often in the shop and leaked radiator fluid at our feet.

After a few years went by, my income soared, our credit score improved, and we settled for a brand-new Subaru wagon as the family car. It was not our dream car, but it was certainly reliable and very practical. Throughout this time, we also had our other beater car, plus at one point a beater truck that my son drove. Then one day I had an epiphany.

Considering that I had written the book *Creating Your Own Destiny* with a subtitle of *How to Get Exactly What You Want Out of Life and Work*, I realized that we only live life once, so what sense did it make to "settle" in life when we can absolutely "choose" our destinies and get exactly what we want. On that same day, I saw a television ad for cars.com and vehix.com, advising me that I could get the exact used car I wanted, with the exact mileage and color I wanted.

I immediately thought that if I could find a blue 9-5 Saab, then I could get rid of the beater and have my son drive the Subaru, and I could again drive the Saab we had never wanted to give up in the first place. So I went online and after a few weeks of searching, I found exactly what I wanted: a 2001 blue Saab 9-5, with sunroof, beige leather heated seats, and 65,000 miles on it, located just north of Seattle. The asking price was only $5,400 and absolutely nothing was wrong with it other than it needed new tires. I called up the seller, made plans to meet with her, withdrew 54 $100 bills from my business account, and went over on a ferryboat to meet her. When I test-drove it, it purred like a kitten. I made the purchase, brought it home, and there sat my Saab in my driveway after a five-year absence. I felt my third child had come home.

What is important to note about this experience is that I have never been one to value material things—because they come and go. What I do value is love, relationships, and family above all else. However, the process of getting back virtually the exact same car, but one year newer, represented to me that my struggling for the previous three or four years to transition from being a dependent employee to an independent entrepreneur was now over! I had successfully made the transition, gotten exactly what I wanted, and now the blue Saab 9-5 represented that if I were willing to believe in my visions, and work day and night for my dreams and goals, then all things in life would work their way out and I could successfully provide for my family, without having a job!

Equally important, I could provide for my clients as a professional speaker and publishing coach, and make a fantastic living, while still pursuing the life of my dreams.

As a result of getting this car back, my former wife took it over as her car, and I was left driving the family Subaru again. With that being the case, I decided I wanted to reward her for sticking with me through all of the tough times, from a perfect credit score and a six-figure job, to a dinged credit score and no job, to now finally, a repaired credit score, a thriving business, and being on the road to becoming an Affluent Entrepreneur.

Once and for all I wanted to make it right so in the summer of 2010, I started working on a special project that could change our financial future. My family could soon work out of choice instead of having to work out of need. The proper execution of the special project could make up for all of the blood, sweat, and tears that we have shed pursuing our goals and dreams. Every once in a lifetime, an opportunity comes along and we either blink and miss it, or we keep our eyes wide open and our lives end up changing forever. This special project has proven to be one of those life-changing events financially for our family, and you too can reap financial rewards if you keep an open mind about this opportunity. This special project is allowing me to build a lasting asset for my family and you can do the same. If you partner with me, I can assure you that you will gain the financial means to secure your family's financial future and achieve your destiny in any economic climate. To learn more about the special project that has changed our lives, and to see whether the same can happen for you, visit www .Numis1.com/PatrickSnow.

I share with you this long story for a couple of reasons. First and foremost, never forgot those important people in your life who stick with you through thick and thin. These are the people you need to reward in one way or another for their loyalty to you in your entrepreneurial quests. These gifts of financial peace of mind can make your relationships even stronger.

Two, the Affluent Entrepreneur is "affluent" because he or she does not throw away money by purchasing depreciating assets. He or she purchases used cars but invests money in assets such as real estate or other investments that increase in value over time.

Third, sometimes you need to reward yourself or your family as you progress, evolve, and become the Affluent Entrepreneur you were born to become. Don't sacrifice your whole life savings because someday you will want it so you can take that trip to Tahiti, build your dream home, and reward your spouse for his or her sacrifices. Turn that someday into today. Live your life to the full and create win-win relationships for all of your loved ones in your life: both your family and your clients.

EXERCISE

List three things you can do for those loved ones in your life who have stood beside you through thick and thin as you have made the transition from employee to entrepreneur:

1. _____

2. _____

3. _____

AFFLUENT ENTREPRENEUR PROFILE
RICHARD BRANSON

A perfect example of a win-win business model is British industrialist Richard Branson who is best known for his Virgin Brand in records, airplanes, and many other industries. Branson has been an entrepreneur his whole life, beginning at age 16 when he started his own magazine called *Student*. He is most widely known for his success in the airline business when he launched Virgin Atlantic Airways along with Virgin Records in the 1980s.

The major challenge Branson had in running an airline was constantly managing cash flow to ensure that all of his plans and ventures could remain afloat, or "airborne." In 1992, when a recession hit awful hard, it became virtually impossible for entrepreneurs to access loans to get lines of credit. Branson had the idea to install in-flight entertainment for all of his passengers (both first class and coach) by adding seatback video terminal technology in all of his planes. To make this happen, he figured he needed $10 million. Since he couldn't get a bank to loan him the money, he nervously called the CEO of Boeing, Phil Condit, and asked him if he were to place an order for 10 new 747 aircraft, would Boeing install these seat-back flight entertainment systems in all 10 of the aircraft? Boeing agreed to do so. As a result, Branson was so excited that he called Jean Pierson of Airbus and asked the same question. Airbus also agreed.

While Branson was unsuccessful in his attempt to raise $10 million for this new technology, he found it easier to get a $4 billion line of credit from the banks to purchase 18 new aircraft. As a result, Virgin Atlantic soon had the newest, youngest fleet of planes, with the best in-flight entertainment available at the time, and Branson had purchased these planes at the cheapest price he had ever been able to acquire planes.

Bottom line, it was a huge win for both Boeing and Airbus because it helped them beat the recession in 1992, and it was a win for Branson because he was able to improve his fleet of planes, while providing the best in-flight entertainment options for his customers. Today, Richard Branson now runs over 300 companies and has amassed a net worth close to $4 billion due to his win-win business models.

EXERCISE

Think for a moment about Richard Branson's example, and then write down three ideas you have that will allow you to access seed money and provide a win-win situation for all those involved.

1. _____
   _____
   _____

2. _____
   _____
   _____

3. _____
   _____
   _____

SUMMARY

Your prospects' favorite radio station is probably the same station you listen to: WIFM (What's In it For Me). Creating win-win opportunities for your business is all about solving problems and easing pain for your prospects. Therefore, you must think outside of the box and ask yourself how can you roll up your sleeves, volunteer extra time (as in the case of working at Subway) to feel your customers' pain, walk a mile in their shoes, and go the extra mile to help them achieve their goals.

What's important to note is that win-win is not just for your prospects and customers. Win-win can be a very strong part of your family. For example, if your children get good grades, you may want to reward them somehow. If you have dragged your family through the mud and dinged the family's credit score, it might not be a bad idea to reward them for their loyalty, belief, and support by purchasing something special to show them how much you love them.

Win-win can take many forms, including even stuffing registration packets with a meeting planner prior to the speech the next day. I ask you to think outside of your box, and see what you can do differently to affect those clients around you. If Richard Branson can secure $4 billion in credit to buy 18 commercial airplanes easier than he can borrow $10 million, then think about all that is possible in your business once you put your clients' needs above yours and you always conduct your business with a win-win mentality.

Leveraging Technology and the Internet

Give me a lever long enough and a prop strong enough,
and I can single-handedly move the world.
—Archimedes

I n this chapter, you will learn a few strategies for leveraging technology and the Internet that will assist you in building the foundation for creating a successful business and becoming an Affluent Entrepreneur. You will also read examples of entrepreneurs who have used these strategies to expand their reach and build their business. Finally, you will see how "The Donald," Mr. Trump, effectively uses technology continuously to build his empire.

Without question, this principle is one of the most essential in this book because technology has revolutionized the way business is done, and it is largely the way business is now done. I'm going to share with you here how to use e-mail, social networking, and search engine optimization (SEO) to your advantage. If you don't want to devote time to executing these strategies effectively, you will learn how to find talented experts to handle them for you. What's important to note is that you don't have to know how all this technology works; you only need to understand why you (or the person to whom you delegate these tasks) must leverage the Internet and technology to your benefit. By taking advantage of these wonderful tools, you will be able to market your business on a global basis around the clock, every day of the year, and then experience the wonder of making money while you sleep!

CONFERENCE CALLS

As a publishing, book marketing, and speaking coach, I have well over 250 clients, and that number continues to grow month after month. As a result, I am often asked how I manage this growth and still provide personal service to all my clients. Well, one of the biggest tools I use, and I encourage you to use as an Affluent Entrepreneur, is the power of conference calls.

I host a Monday morning 8 AM PST Inner Circle Publishing Mastermind call every week, as I have been doing for years. This call is for my publishing, book marketing, and speaking clients. See, the cool thing about a conference call to me is that it does not matter whether there are 10 people on the call or 1,000 people; it takes me just one hour of time to host the call, yet if there are 25 people on the line, then that saves me 25 hours of individual coaching time by phone with 25 of my clients. Each caller dials in with questions . . . and the beautiful thing is that I do not need to be prepared for the call because after 15 years in this industry, I have personally discovered and learned almost every answer to every question the callers have. Even better, each caller gets to listen to the questions from the other dialers along with my answers, and then apply this new knowledge to their lives. As a result, it is a win-win for all involved.

E-MAIL

I give all of my clients unlimited e-mail access to me because I can more quickly answer their questions that way than trying to schedule one-on-one time with all of them. In addition, I can reply to them when it is convenient to me rather than having to field a bunch of phone calls throughout the day, or trying to call them back with answers, only to end up playing phone tag.

Despite e-mail's advantages, however, it does have its challenges. First, people are often inundated with spam and also personal e-mails, so the sheer volume of e-mail makes it difficult to sift through and determine which e-mails are priorities and need immediate responses, which ones can wait for later, and which ones just to delete without reading. And the more successful your business becomes, the greater the e-mail volume you are going to see.

To solve this dilemma, I recommend you either have an assistant filter through your e-mail, or you set up a folder system so all incoming e-mails are automatically filtered to one of your preset folders.

An additional difficulty is that with Facebook and other social networking sites, there are other ways besides e-mail for people to send you communications. To combat this issue, on these social networking sites where I have my profile page and my "follow me" links, I have a section that says, "e-mail preferred." That way if visitors plan on contacting me, they will be encouraged to use e-mail since that is I how I prefer to communicate. Therefore, if you as the reader want to get in touch with me, the best way is to send me an e-mail at: Patrick@PatrickSnow.com. In addition, you might also delegate having your assistant who monitors your e-mail also stay up to date on your social networking sites for you.

BLOGGING

Blogging is a fantastic way to get your message out into the marketplace. However, the challenge here is the time it takes to write your own blog and create a large following of readers. When promoting the Wiley release of my first book *Creating Your Own Destiny*, I learned about how to build a following from a pioneer in the industry. In his book *The New Rules of Marketing and PR*, David Meerman Scott talks about how the media is completely changing the way everything is done on the Internet, and more specifically, how authors' strategies are changing so they can better market their books.

In the olden days, authors would publish a book and then blast e-mails out to their clients and to their list in hopes that people would purchase their books. This worked in the beginning, but it does not work anymore. Additionally, authors would e-mail or fax press releases to journalists in hopes that these journalists would actually go out of their way to write a story on their books. Well, the problem there is two-fold: (1) The journalist often does not get to select the exact subject matter he or she writes about. Many times journalists have bosses or managing editors who decide what content is produced by that newspaper or magazine, and (2) Journalists' in-boxes are flooded with hundreds of press releases that have been sent to them. Not to mention that the amount of mail received by journalists is also overwhelming.

Long story short, David Meerman Scott realized there had to be a better way for authors to be seen and heard. His idea was to get bloggers involved in the equation, so he amassed a list of 150 of the largest bloggers in North America who blogged on his subject matter (social media and public relations). He then sent a review copy of his book, *The New Rules of Marketing and PR*, to the bloggers on the list, asking them to blog about his book.

His results were absolutely stunning. In roughly the first 90 days, he sold thousands of books and hit the bestseller lists. With *Creating Your Own Destiny*, I applied David's wisdom and strategy to my book. In the process, I realized a couple of things.

First, yes, it is important to be active in social networking and to develop thousands of followers and friends. But no matter how many friends we attract (unless you are Ashton Kutcher, whom I understand has more followers than anyone on the planet), you will never be able to attract as many fans and friends as the top bloggers in your area already have reading their blogs. My thoughts were that since bloggers oftentimes work from home and rarely get large volumes of mail, they can actually select the subject matters they write about and determine when to write about it, so David Meerman Scott's strategy was pure genius.

Secondly, I discovered the one flaw in this strategy. Why would anyone blog about my book without my doing anything in return? I could have solved that problem by starting my own blog and blogging about the other bloggers, thereby returning the favor, but I did not want to get into the blog space and try to compete for readers. I concluded that it made more sense for me to be a matchmaker, a resource for existing bloggers, and to create a link on my site called "Cool Blogs." Next I would add each blogger's name, blog address, and subject matter to my site and promote his or her book and blog to my large list subscribers. Next, I would show this link on my page to these bloggers, and finally, I would follow up with a review copy of my book and cover letter asking them to help me out, just as I had done for them.

Bottom line, I do something for them by promoting their blogs, and in return, they promote my book, thereby creating a win-win situation. When *Creating Your Own Destiny* was republished by John Wiley & Sons, Inc., in April 2010, my results of leveraging other people's blogs resulted in the sale of thousands of books.

FAN PAGES AND SOCIAL NETWORKING ADS

Next, due to the red-hot growth experienced by Facebook, I took this strategy to the next level. I started microblogging from my fan page by sending out a daily two- to three-line inspirational quote from my book in an attempt to inspire all of those who had joined my fan page. The way it works is that I post one small quote/entry on my fan page, which is automatically placed on the page of all those fans. Once I set up my fan page, literally in a few short months, I had thousands of fans enjoying and passing on these inspirational quotes. Each day in an attempt to brand both my book cover and my photo, I would alternate these images used in my communications.

To become a fan of my Facebook page, simply go to my site www.PatrickSnow.com and then scroll down and join my fan page, or visit http://www.facebook.com/TheDeanOfDestiny.

If Facebook were a country, it would be the fourth-largest country in the world—it has over 400 million members at the time I am writing this book, and by the time you read these words, it will probably be in the half a billion range. Due to the vast number of people on Facebook and my desire as an author to build my brand and sell more books, I wanted to investigate how social networking ads worked. At the nudging of my buddy, Denny Andrews, I decided to test market some Facebook ads and commit to spending $15 per day on this site and then measure the results after seven days.

The results absolutely shocked me. My ads were for book sales, publishing coaching, and speaking engagements. I placed about seven ads in total and set my advertising budget to $10 per day ($300 per month). After forty-five days and $450 invested, 2.3 million impressions of the book cover led to 800 click-throughs to my web site. The results were a bunch of books being sold and $5,000 from coaching clients coming my way. The actual cost to do this ad for that timeframe was $450. Trading $450 for $5,000 and having over 2 million people see my book cover—that is the best deal going.

Needless to say, I have decided to continue with my Facebook ads as a permanent part of my marketing strategy moving forward.

THE INTERNET

Small business owners often ask me what is the best resource available today to find buyers for your products or services. My answer is simple—and there is only one resource that deserves this kind of praise and recognition: the Internet. The Internet is the single greatest resource available today that can easily give you access to finding all of your customers.

In a previous chapter, I introduced you to my VP of Sales Mary West. Well, Mary is nothing less than brilliant; she consistently surprises me with new ways to leverage the Internet to find more business. A recent strategy she used resulted in tens of thousands of dollars in revenue for my business. Mary is constantly trying to identify meeting planners who are looking to book world-class speakers to entertain their audiences at conferences throughout the world.

To make a long story short, Mary Googled "Speaker Bureaus." A speaker bureau is an organization that has a database of speakers and is constantly trying to match its speakers with meeting planners. To make this match happen, the speaker bureau is paid a commission fee for its time. Well, Mary stumbled across one speaker bureau on the Internet and then looked at its list of speakers. The cool thing about this site was she could read testimonials for each of the speakers along with their bios. Meeting planners, who had paid big money to book these speakers, wrote all the testimonials.

Well, Mary stumbled across a speaker who apparently had spoken for Subway, the giant franchiser of fresh deli sandwiches. Mary read the name of the meeting planner from Subway who wrote a glorious testimonial for this particular speaker. With this name in hand, Mary then Googled the meeting planner's name and the address for Subway's world headquarters. She found the name, phone number, and address, all online. The meeting planner was located in Milton, Connecticut, and since I was going to be traveling to Connecticut soon, it was perfect timing.

You already know the rest of the story, which I told in an earlier chapter. In short, Subway booked me to speak in Chicago later that summer for thousands of dollars. This opportunity wouldn't have happened if Mary had not leveraged the Internet. Subway is just one example of many, many speaking engagements Mary West has found for me, by leveraging the Internet.

EXERCISE

List five ways you as an Affluent Entrepreneur can leverage the Internet to find more clients online.

1. _____

_____

_____

2. _____
   _____
   _____

3. _____
   _____
   _____

4. _____
   _____
   _____

5. _____
   _____
   _____

AFFLUENT ENTREPRENEUR PROFILE
DONALD TRUMP

After graduating from the Wharton School of Business at the University of Pennsylvania in 1968, Donald Trump joined his father's real estate company to work on middle-income housing units in Queens. In 1971, he moved to Manhattan where he felt greater opportunity existed and bigger real estate investment deals could be made.

As the market boomed, Trump took on high-profile projects such as the Trump Tower on New York's Fifth Avenue and the Taj Mahal Casino Resort in Atlantic City. After some financial setbacks and two high-profile divorces, Trump rebounded stronger than ever with more high-end real estate ventures in Manhattan, the reality TV show *The Apprentice*, and numerous best-selling business, real estate, and entrepreneurship books.

Throughout this time, Trump continued to leverage the Internet and technology by launching the very successful Trump University, an online education company, to teach others about real estate investing. He also made history by personally endorsing ACN (the world's largest direct seller of telecommunication services), which markets several products including a very popular video phone so you can see the person with whom you are speaking on the other line. These are just two examples of the many ventures Donald Trump is personally involved with that all have one thing in common: All drive revenue to his company as a result of his leveraging technology and the Internet.

Trump's many entrepreneurial activities throughout his lifetime have amassed for him a net worth of $2 billion. More important, he has influenced the lives and business strategies of millions of other entrepreneurs through real estate dealings, his television program, and his numerous best-selling books.

SUMMARY

Without question, if you want to become an Affluent Entrepreneur, you must do everything possible to keep up with all the changes going on around you in the technology sector. Keep an open mind. If you don't understand a technology, let others explain not only how it works, but more important, how the technology can work for your company and your financial gain. Once you comprehend what is happening, you can take action and leverage all the technology, information, and communication capabilities the Internet has to offer to better position yourself and your company to be exposed to the billions of people online.

The Internet is the best tool you can have in your arsenal. Once you learn to leverage it to work for you, you will become an Affluent Entrepreneur.

Taking Calculated Risks

> The world stands aside to let anyone pass
> who knows where he is going.
> —David Starr Jordan

In this chapter, you will learn what you should and shouldn't risk, and when the time is right to take those risks. Sometimes, it's not easy to decide. For example, you should never be willing to risk your faith or your family in the pursuit of your business. However, there are times when you should risk your credit, your money, your investment portfolio, and your database for your business's success. You'll discover how to minimize your exposure to potential failure by taking calculated, well-thought-out risks that significantly increase your chances of success. You'll also read how an American Oil Tycoon, II. L. Hunt, risked his money and future for his passion, and you'll learn whether or not it paid off for him.

RISK

If you were to look up "risk" in the dictionary, it would be defined as: *Exposure to the chance of injury or loss.*

My definition of a "calculated risk" is: *Minimum exposure to the chance of emotional injury or financial loss due to your due diligence, research, and dogged determination to make your venture work no matter what the obstacle or adversity standing in your way.*

How do you like those definitions? I like the second one better. I am not one to take foolish risks such as skydiving. I have no desire ever to jump out of an airplane, but I certainly would if the plane was going to crash. My point is there is a huge difference between taking risks and taking calculated risks. Gamblers risk their money at casinos, and most of the time they lose. Affluent Entrepreneurs, on the other hand, take calculated risks and win more times than not.

I have taken two major calculated risks in my life, and both paid off in a large way. Let me explain. When I was 18 years old, I was a freshman at Albion College, attending school on a football grant/financial aid package. Albion College was a Division III school with a solid football program. Since it was my dream to play in the NFL, and because I was too small to play at the Division I level as a late bloomer, I settled for Albion College. Well, to make a long story short, I had a career-ending back injury that took about 3–6 months of rehabilitation before I could fully recover.

The problem was, at the time, I let other people's opinions of me determine my reality. As we talked about earlier in this book, it was Les Brown who said, "Never let someone else's opinion of you determine your reality!" Today, I have made this mantra become part of my everyday life. However, at 18 years old I had not yet heard this invaluable advice. So when the team doctor said I could never play football again, I believed him.

If I have any regret in life, it is that I never made a comeback to play the game I love. Now in my forties, I am big enough to play in the NFL, but I'm just too old. In fact, for years when my kids were very young, they believed for a short time that the only reason their father didn't make it to the NFL was due to an injury. What a great time we had when my boys were young and believed everything I told them. Now that my sons are teenagers, they are quick to remind me of all of those things I don't know yet.

My point is that I believed the team doctor. Having lost my dream, I was at a crossroads in my life. I started soul-searching, trying to imagine what the next chapter of my life could look like. I took an inventory of my passions and was quick to comprehend that after football, my next greatest passions were mountain biking and skiing. So I decided to transfer to one of the best schools in the Rocky Mountains that was closest to places where I could pursue skiing and mountain biking—the University of Montana in Missoula. I applied there, was accepted, and transferred just after the winter break. I was back on the track to starting my life all over again.

I have always been so grateful to my parents for all their support as I followed my visions. However, before I left Michigan, I went to visit my grandmother, Christine Snow, in Flint. She cooked me up my favorite dinner and spoiled me with her fantastic apple pie for dessert. Then as I said my goodbyes, I gave her a big kiss and hug at the entrance of her house. She continued to hug me and wouldn't let me go. I noticed tears in her eyes. When I asked her what was wrong, she replied, "Patrick, you think you are just going out West to school, but I know in my heart what will happen. You will settle down and live out West the rest of your life." I shrugged off her foresight of the future and went on my way.

Looking back on this experience, she was so right! I married my college sweetheart just before graduation, moved to Seattle, had two boys, and started our life together, never moving back to Michigan. It is amazing to look back and see how wise my grandmother really was. I am so grateful to have selected the career of being a professional speaker because for the last 2–3 years of my grandmother's life, I was fortunate enough to book a half-dozen speaking engagements in Michigan, and with each trip, I made sure I stopped by the senior assisted center to visit her. She and my parents have been such a huge impact on my life by encouraging me to follow my dreams and never trying to hold me back.

Calculated risk number one was starting my life all over again at 18 years old and moving out West not knowing a single soul on that side of the Mississippi.

Calculated risk number two was the decision to follow my passions, my dreams, and my love for speaking. At this point in my life, I had two young boys and a very stable job in corporate sales.

Exercise A

Looking back at your life, what are three of the biggest risks you have taken in regards to your family and your career?

1. _____

2. _____

3. _____

However, I continued to moonlight on the side as a speaker. From 22–26 years old, I gave an estimated 300 speeches to Rotary, Kiwanis, FBLA, DECA, churches, schools, and anyone who would suffer through passionate talks that seemed to be disorganized but yet were full of energy. I look back now and realize that I needed those 300 trial-and-error speeches to get better and improve. For speaking, I got free breakfast, free lunch, free dinner, and every now and then, I would get lucky and score a free pen or a free mug.

After years of frustration wondering why I could not turn my hobby of speaking into a business of speaking, I had a "Come to Jesus" talk due to my Christian faith. The answer I got back was that if I wanted what others have, I must be willing to do what others have done. I looked at my mentors, all the best professional speakers of the time—Les Brown, Zig Ziglar, Brian Tracy, Tony Robbins, and Dr. Stephen Covey—and asked what they all had in common. The answer was that each one had successfully self-published his book, and it was his book that stood as his platform from which he launched his professional speaking business.

I knew right then and there that I needed to do the same if I was to achieve my goal of becoming a professional speaker. I will never forget my former wife's response when I told her I was going to write a book. She said, "Patrick, who are you to write a book? You don't have a Super Bowl ring on your finger, or an Olympic Gold Medal hanging from your neck, and you haven't climbed Mount Everest!" Her questions hit home, making me realize I needed to come up with those answers of just what made me qualified to write a book. The answer was that I was an everyday person with a vision and a determination to succeed, and I knew that if I could do it, I could prove that anyone could do it. To this day I thank my former wife for her lack of faith in me that only inspired me further to pursue my goals and achieve my destiny.

So there I was, willing to risk my entire sales career and future as an "employee" to pursue this passion of speaking by writing and publishing a book. I knew that I could minimize my level of risk and protect my family if I kept my day job as long as I could while moonlighting as a speaker and writer.

I looked at my sales career and thought, *I guess it is possible to make a decent career as a sales professional, but I will always have a boss looking over my shoulder and always be concerned about someone else creating the product or the service. Or, I can risk my short-term financial wellbeing and make the needed investment of both time and money to make a go of it as a professional speaker.* To make a long story short, I spent five years of my life and $20,000 getting the first version of my book, *Creating Your Own Destiny*, published. It was far from perfect—there were several grammar errors inside plus on the back cover the word "freedom" was misspelled with three "eee's" as "freeedom," but I had still succeeded in my goal, and I knew I could always improve it with successive printings, and I have done just that.

The book was published in July of 2001, and just a few months later because of 9/11 and other industry changes, my life was turned upside down when eight days later, I was laid off, fired, let go, downsized—whatever word you want to use—the result is the same. I was no longer earning my six-figure income from my sales position selling printed circuit boards. I remember driving north on I-5 heading home after the fateful meeting at Starbucks where my boss gave me the news. All the printed circuit board manufacturing was moving offshore to China because in China employees on the shop floor were willing to work for $30 per month, while our workers in the United States wanted $4,000–$5,000 per month.

I fully understood the situation, but what frustrated me the most was that another person, another organization, and/or the reality of the new economy were in control of my financial ability to provide for my family. As a result of these events, I made a decision on that drive home, that never again would I ever risk my ability to provide for my family by being an employee who depended on someone else for income. And I hoped that now my "calculated risk" was going to pay off for me since I had published my book.

However, my problem was that I was not yet in a financial position to make the transition full-time into the speaking business, even though my book had just been published. So, I took another sales position in the circuit board industry, but from the first day of that job, I knew it wouldn't work because of the offshore moves being made in the industry. As I expected, in 2002, I was again let go. Strike two. What next?

My only obvious choice was to go full-time into the speaking business, but I was still virtually an unknown. I persisted anyway and moved forward to build my speaking career; at the time, it felt as though it took forever to replace that six-figure paycheck as a full-time entrepreneur. Thankfully, my former wife had a job as a prosecuting attorney, so during this time of transition, it was her paycheck that kept the lights on, so to speak.

However, with the loss of 50 percent of our income, we got behind on all of our bills. After about 18 months of being in that situation, we had another "Come to Jesus" talk and made the difficult decision that if we sold our family home, we could take the equity from our house, pay off all of our debts (other than school loans), and start over again as renters. So I risked my house for the belief in our vision.

Through this process, I took one last sales job for nine months, and in that nine months my speaking business, book sales, and publishing coaching seemed to skyrocket and take off. As a result, I quit my job at age 36, retired on my own terms, and stuck to my decision never again to let my family's financial future rest in the hands of another organization. Since then, I have not worked a single day, nor plan to ever again for the rest of my life. Sure, I have been building my business all these years, but it is not work when you do what you love.

Calculated risk two paid off, but only after years of blood, sweat, and tears. And now I am free to pursue my own passion, my own destiny, on my own terms, regardless of what the economy is doing. I encourage you to do the same. However, I suggest you keep your day job as long as you can while you are building your business.

As a result of my story, you can see that I risked everything for the pursuit of my passions and my business. I risked my entire investment portfolio. I liquidated it and invested it in my business. I risked my perfect 800 credit score by getting behind on my bills. I risked our family home, by selling it, downsizing to a rental, and then later buying again. I risked virtually everything except the two most important things in my life: my faith and my family. As a result, my faith in God is stronger than ever!

EXERCISE B

With the economy being the way it is, look forward in your life and ask yourself what are some risks that you currently face that you may need to address, head on, in order to protect your family's long-term financial health?

1. _____

2. _____

3. _____

4. _____

5. _____

6. _____

Now in the lines below, write three actions you are going to take immediately as "calculated risks" to do what is in your best interest moving forward. Write down these three actions. I challenge you to take these actions prior to the end of the week!

1. _____

_____

_____

2. _____

_____

_____

3. _____

_____

_____

AFFLUENT ENTREPRENEUR PROFILE
H. L. HUNT

Even today, H. L. Hunt is still considered by many to be the foremost American Oil Tycoon. His whole life he was a gambler, with poker as his game of choice. After being raised in Illinois, he settled in Arkansas where in 1912 he was running a cotton plantation. When floods from the Mississippi River ruined his crops, he quickly turned to poker to support his family. He was willing to take risks in games, life, business, and with his family. He had 14 children in total. He had children with his first wife and the mistress he had on the side, and then with his second mistress, who became his second wife after his first wife died. His first wife apparently never knew about the mistresses (talk about risky).

Soon thereafter, he was attracted to the oil business. He started out by trading in oil leases, buying and selling land for other people without spending a penny of his own money. Eventually, he expanded his business to start oil drilling in both Oklahoma and Louisiana. In 1930, Hunt partnered with a veteran of the oil drilling business, a guy by the name of Joiner, who had been unsuccessful in his last 17 attempts at finding large reserves of oil. Joiner found himself deep in debt, and the bank wanted its money back on the loans made to him on the oil drilling equipment.

Hunt, however, did his research and found that Joiner had stumbled across a potentially very large oil field. The risks faced by Hunt were astronomical, but he believed that Joiner was sitting on a geological gold mine. Therefore, Hunt offered Joiner $50,000 in cash and $45,000 in notes plus a guarantee of $1.3 million based on the production of this land in future oil proceeds. As a result of this payout strategy, Hunt pioneered the term "production payment" in the oil industry, a term still used today.

Hunt's risk paid off when an underground lake of oil was discovered at this location, estimated to be 9 miles wide, and over 40 miles long. At the time, it was the biggest oil find the world had ever seen. H. L. Hunt was rewarded with a share of the profits, conservatively estimated as a payout to him of roughly $100 million. Not bad for a poker player who did his homework, evaluated the opportunity, and took the calculated risk to benefit from the return on his investment. Upon Hunt's death in 1974, his net worth was estimated to be between $2 billion and $3 billion, and he was making about $1 million a day.

SUMMARY

My point about taking calculated risks is this: No one on this planet will become an Affluent Entrepreneur unless he or she is able to evaluate risk, take calculated risks, and then eventually burn his bridges and move forward to pursue his destiny on his own terms. If you are serious about becoming an Affluent Entrepreneur, I encourage you to take calculated risks in order to protect and provide for your family for the long haul.

It has been said that so many people fail in life because they quit digging just a feet inches shy of their gold mines. I believe the true risk in life is giving up and accepting mediocrity. I challenge you to take an inventory of your passions, determine which passions are the most marketable, and then spend the rest of your life taking calculated risks. By doing so, I assure you that sooner or later you will strike gold, find oil, or achieve your revenue goals.

My fellow speaker and friend Mike Dugan has always said that "Fortune favors the bold; no risk no reward."

So take risks, spice up your life, live your passions, and as a result, you will never work another day of your life because when you are doing what you love, it is not work, it is play!

PRINCIPLE 12

Turning Adversity into Your University

Obstacles are necessary for success because in selling
as in all careers of importance, victory comes only
after many struggles and countless defeats.
—Og Mandino

In this chapter, you will discover that the only way to fail is to stop
pursuing your goals and dreams. If you keep moving toward your
goals, then you can't fail. Brian Tracy, my mentor, friend, and
business partner, constantly tells me that we simply don't have
enough time in our lives to learn all we need to learn to be
successful. That's why we need to reduce our learning curve by
studying the successes and failures of others. Then we can avoid the
failures when possible and emulate the successes as we advance
toward our own success. This principle will help you better
understand that all the setbacks in your life and in your business
have made you a better entrepreneur, more capable of navigating
any rough waters ahead. Another mentor and friend, Art Mortell,
taught me there's no such thing as failure—just experiences that
end up producing undesired results. I will show you how to harness
these lessons, which will make it easier for you to achieve success in
your business. You also will learn how family plays a very important
role in sticking together to beat adversity. You'll learn about the
trials and tribulations of Abraham Lincoln, and finally, you'll be
inspired by how Oprah Winfrey turned around a rough start in life
to become an inspiration for us all.

FAILURE

So many people are afraid of failure because they think that if they attempt something and fail, it will mean the end of life, or the world will cease to exist. This is not true! Bottom line, I think what you and others may be worried about is this: "What will other people think of me if I attempt something and I get a less than desirable result, or if I fall flat on my face?" My response is, "Who cares what others think about you? All that matters is what you think of yourself." I have said it before, and I will say it again, using speaker and author Les Brown's words, "Never let another person's opinion of you become your reality."

You see, sticking to a normal life—a life without risk—is boring. So many people think they will opt for the safe and secure way and just keep their job and not attempt any new venture on their own. In other words, they just want to be given fish on payday rather than choosing to learn to fish for themselves. This mind-set is very, very dangerous because, once they lose their jobs, they will literally starve.

What about you? Do you have what it takes to risk the safe route and pursue entrepreneurship? I believe that since you are reading this book and you have gotten this far without putting it down, you do! I think you are more talented than you realize, and if you continue reading this book to the end, I will arm you with enough tackle for "fishing" that you will be able to tackle any obstacle, fish for yourself, and eat whatever you want.

One of my close friends and business partners Thach Nguyen is authoring the book *Wealth by Default*. Thach writes that most people cannot grow if they don't experience adversity. An immigrant from Vietnam, Thach and his family came to the United States when he was just a young boy. Today, he is a multimillionaire because he has overcome all the adversity that has come his way.

When Thach and his family were escaping from Vietnam, they almost missed the last plane out of Saigon. His father packed up all their family's belongings in their family vehicle. Then their vehicle broke down on the way to the airport so their family was stuck overnight. His father made the long walk into the nearest town and came back to fix their vehicle; they just barely made it in time for the last flight.

As a result, Thach has a personal mantra I think we should all live by. It goes like this, "You can't have a breakthrough in your life until you go through a breakdown." At 9/11, my family had a breakdown when I lost my high-tech sales job due to downsizing. When I again lost my job in 2002, my family had another break-down. As a result of these experiences, I was able to have a breakthrough and dive into my speaking, book, and coaching business full-time. As a family we then made a breakthrough, and now I will never again have to work for anyone else the rest of my life. How about you?

A FEW OF MY ADVERSITIES

Numerous times in my life adversity has strengthened my character as a person and my resolves as an entrepreneur. The first one came when I was 13 years old and a drunk driver crashed into the side of our family home and destroyed the natural gas line on the side of our house, which caused an instant explosion and a house fire that took approximately 90 minutes for the firefighters to extinguish.

My family was left without a place to live for the summer so we bounced around. That first night, we slept on the floor of the church across the street. Then we moved into a hotel called the Presidential Arms for three or four nights (believe you me, there was nothing presidential about that place). Next, we moved to a motel near a grocery store parking lot for a week. Finally, my parents found us a rental home for three months while our house was being rebuilt. One blessing was that this house had a swimming pool so it made the summer more enjoyable. My takeaway from this lesson was that if you have love and the togetherness of your family, then that is all you need.

Next, several years later in my early thirties, after being laid off meant the loss of my six-figure income, I fell behind on our mortgage payments and credit cards, so much so that I completely stopped making payments on my credit cards so that I could pay for the basic necessities of food, clothing, and shelter for my family. Once behind on my mortgage, I negotiated a "catch-up" payment plan with the bank, which meant I now had to make a mortgage payment and a half for nine months to catch up and prevent any chance of a foreclosure on my home. Therefore, I paid approximately $4,000 a month for eight consecutive months, and was closer than ever to getting caught up and getting my finances back to normal. I had just done another speaking engagement and deposited $5,000 into my bank account the day before my ninth catch-up mortgage payment was due. I called my mortgage company and authorized them electronically to take their payment and all was good. That day, I remember thinking "I did it" and that the tough times were over.

To my surprise, the next day I received a call from the mortgage bank telling me there were "insufficient funds" in my account to cover this last catch-up payment. I thought there had to be an error so I rushed down to my local bank to see what had happened. It turned out that one of the credit card companies that I hadn't paid for quite some time had secured a "judgment" against me, allowing them access to go into my bank account and withdraw funds without needing permission from me. This credit card company had taken that $5,000 deposit right out from under me.

There I was, sitting in my home office, never before having cried as an adult except at my grandmother's funeral. There I sat, a grown man, crying, disgusted with our circumstances, shameful, embarrassed, having no idea of what to do or where to turn. A grown man crying feels like a failure. I will never forget that day; it burned so deeply that it fueled my entrepreneurial fire like no other event in my life. I decided that day that I would make it through this adversity "No Matter What." I remember thinking that in life, either things "will" happen to you that often you can't control, or you "WILL" things to happen out of sure determination. Well, I "WILLED" things to happen. My family and I decided to sell our home, take the equity from it, and downsize into a smaller home. Over time, everything worked out for the better. The bottom line again was that as an adult (just as my parents did during the summer of our house fire), I went the extra mile to make absolutely sure my family all stayed together.

When you keep your faith and your family as a top priority, you learn to stick together, and as a family unit, a team, you become stronger together than if you were apart. During your times of financial crisis, I encourage you to stick together, whether it means sleeping on a church floor, in a rundown hotel, or in a strange house you don't own. You will make it through and become a stronger family unit as the result of your adversity.

PRESIDENTIAL EXAMPLE

Adversity just doesn't happen to everyday common people; it also happens to presidents. Such was the case for Abraham Lincoln. Look at the timeline below for an example of how every time he got knocked down, he got right back up again. You too need to do the same, regardless of your adversity:

Abraham Lincoln Timeline

1831	He failed in business.
1832	He was defeated for the state legislature.
1833	He failed again in business.
1835	His sweetheart died.
1836	He suffered from a severe mental breakdown.
1838	He was defeated as speaker of the state legislature.
1846	He was elected to Congress (but lost the 1848 re-election).
1855	He was defeated for the Senate.
1856	He was defeated for the Vice Presidency.
1858	He was again defeated for the Senate.
1860	He was elected as the sixteenth President of the United States of America.

What are you going to do the next time you get knocked down? My challenge and hope for you is that you will get right back up again. It does not matter how many times you fall—all that matters is that you rise one more time than you fall.

QUOTES TO HELP YOU BEAT ADVERSITY

Following are a few quotes I have used as resources to help me overcome any and all hard times that have come my way.

"When you come to the end of your rope, tie a knot and hold on."
—*Eleanor Roosevelt, First Lady*

"That which does not kill, strengthens."
—*Friedrich Nietzsche, German philosopher*

"I have missed over 9,000 shots in my career. I have lost almost 300 games. Twenty-six times I've been trusted to take the game winning shot . . . and missed. I have failed over and over again in my life, and that is why I have succeeded."
—*Michael Jordan, six-time NBA Champion,*
All-Star MVP, one of the 50 greatest players
in NBA history, and Olympic gold medalist
basketball player

EXERCISE A

What breakdowns are you currently facing that are causing a tremendous amount of adversity in your life?

1. _____
   _____
   _____

2. _____
   _____
   _____

3. _____
   _____
   _____

4. _____
   _____
   _____

5. _____
   _____
   _____

Exercise B

What lessons or silver lining can you find or discover as a result? Which of these breakdowns are actually allowing you to have breakthroughs in your life?

1. _____
   _____
   _____

2. _____
   _____
   _____

3. _____
   _____
   _____

4. _____
   _____
   _____

5. _____
   _____
   _____

AFFLUENT ENTREPRENEUR PROFILE
OPRAH WINFREY

Oprah Winfrey was born out of wedlock to teenage parents on January 29, 1954, in Kosciusko, Mississippi. In her early years, Oprah lived with her grandmother who provided her with a solid foundation to overcome the adversity into which she was born. At six years old, Oprah was sent to live with her father and stepmother. At nine, she was raped by a cousin and later molested by others in the community. At 14, she gave birth to a premature baby who did not make it.

Yet with all of these adversities she faced, it would have been easy for her to give up and go in the wrong direction. Not Oprah. She turned these adversities into her university and soon started to excel in her academics, earning a scholarship to study speech and drama at Tennessee State University. She soon became the first African-American news anchor at the TV station in Nashville.

Oprah soon found herself doing a daytime talk show, and *The Oprah Winfrey Show* was born and picked up for national distribution in 1986. Today, her show has been airing for nearly 25 years and reaches close to 50 million viewers in 134 countries. In 1996, she started Oprah's Book Club, which virtually guaranteed up-and-coming authors best-seller status if Oprah selected their books. In 2000, she launched her very own magazine *O, The Oprah Magazine*. She masterminded a reality television show titled *Oprah's Big Give* in 2008. Her company Harpo Productions produces the *Rachael Ray Show* and the *Dr. Phil Show*.

As a result of her turning her adversities into her university, Oprah Winfrey has become a blessing to the world and amassed a net worth of $2.4 billion. But what is most impressive about her is her gigantic heart and her willingness to give and to help others in need. Inspired by Nelson Mandela, the former president of South Africa, Oprah created her *Angel Network* in 1999 with a mission of providing grant money to nonprofit organizations around the world. Most notable is the establishment of her Leadership Academy for Girls in South Africa. Yes indeed, Oprah has certainly beat adversity and become a real angel here on earth and an inspiration for all.

SUMMARY

Always remember that the adversities you face in your life become your university of wisdom and knowledge; through the education of adversity you gain the experience needed for dealing with life's difficulties, and you become more appreciative of its joys. You become a more skilled and wiser captain of your ship as you steer through each wave of adversity, and you then become stronger and more capable of handling future obstacles.

Remember that the breakdowns you experience are really transition points in your life for tremendous breakthroughs. These life experiences will give you the compassion and inspiration to give back to the world as Oprah has done and to make someone else's journey a bit easier.

Whether you realize it or not, you have everything you need to address any and all adversities you face. My challenge to you is to keep your family together through these tough times, and if you do, you will come out on the other end of your adversity stronger than ever and as a more talented Affluent Entrepreneur.

Using Other People's Money

*It's not that I am so smart; it's just that
I stay with problems longer.*
—Albert Einstein

In this chapter, you will learn five ways to raise seed money to fund your business, three of which involve "Other People's Money," often referred to as OPM. Entrepreneurs need to look at creative ways to fund and grow their businesses, and here you will learn how, why, and where to look to find these hidden sources of money. You will also read about the cofounders of Google and see how and where they acquired their angel investment to launch Google.

Let's face it, the problem many small business owners have is that they often lack money and are undercapitalized as a result. This problem needs to be dealt with head on. The best way to do so is to understand, study, and know all the options available to you as you grow your business.

FIVE TYPES OF SEED MONEY

When things seem grim and the bank has turned you down for a loan, don't sweat it—we have all been there. The reality is that you actually have five choices to investigate when it comes to acquiring seed money to help you grow your business.

1. Your day job or business income

2. Your savings or retirement

3. Your credit cards

4. Angel investors who are friends or family

5. Venture capitalists

Each of these options has its advantages and disadvantages. For example, day job income is money you don't have to pay back, but savings are not something everyone has the luxury of having. Credit cards are the bank's money, and they can have high interest rates. The fourth source is angel investors (family, friends, or other business owners), and the fifth option is venture capitalists. In this chapter, we're going to focus primarily on these last two options. As we explore this principle, you'll learn that even if you don't have capital, you can still start a new business or fund your existing business if you use Other People's Money.

BEST SOLUTION

Whenever I have found myself in a position where I have felt I needed operating funds to make my business grow, or even to survive at times, I have always come to the conclusion that yes, while I can borrow money, use a line of credit, or charge things on my credit card, those are not the best solutions.

The best solution is always to go out and sell more of your product or services, to make more sales to drive revenues, to close more deals, and to bring on more clients. When you sell more, you can use the revenue from the sales to foster the growth of your business. Out of 100 times, every single time, actual earned income is always better than taking loans out from others. Read below to see how Henry Ford focused on the revenue part of this equation instead of turning to outside investors. I am so impressed by Mr. Ford's model that it has given me an idea I am running with. Hopefully, this example will equally inspire you to think more creatively about how you can fund your business first through your customers' revenue, and then if this fails, you can consider using Other People's Money (OPM).

Your Most Audacious Goal in Life

What is your biggest, most audacious goal in life? My biggest, most audacious goal is to own my own NFL team! My football team will be called The Hawaii Tiger Sharks (www.HawaiiTigerSharks .com), and we will open operations in Honolulu within 10 years when we raise $2 billion in revenues.

In addition to the required investment capital, we will need to receive the NFL's blessing to purchase an expansion team. Keep in mind that in the eyes of the NFL, cities higher than Honolulu on their depth chart (so to speak) include Los Angeles, London, Toronto, and perhaps even San Antonio. Therefore, how am I going to pull this off, you might ask? Well, I have no idea, but I am pursuing a strategy that I believe may work. I learned this idea from one of the most Affluent Entrepreneurs the world has ever known.

Remember earlier when I talked about how Henry Ford presold automobiles to raise revenue? I intend to do something very similar in nature. My goal is to raise $2 billion in 10 years. One way I intend to raise part of the capital is by selling our Hawaii Tiger Sharks hats for $100 each. For each hat purchased, you will receive a Hawaii Tiger Sharks ticket to a future game ($100 × 20 million hats = $2 billion in seed money).

If for whatever reason, I am unsuccessful in my bid to get an NFL team, you will have purchased a $100 hat and agreed not to take any recourse against my ownership group or me. In the meantime, your $100 Tiger Sharks hat will serve as your daily reminder to pursue your biggest, most audacious goals in life—no matter how bold or fearless they may be.

To purchase your $100 hat and a free ticket to a future Hawaii Tiger Sharks game (within 10–15 years as only a certain number of free tickets can be allocated per each game), visit www.Hawaii TigerSharks.com. There is no limit to the number of hats you may purchase. Thanks for your support, and I challenge you to let your hat serve as your daily reminder to pursue your biggest, most audacious goal in life. If you would like to pay more for your $100 hat, all additional seed money donated is greatly appreciated.

EXERCISE

Now that you know my biggest, most audacious goals in life, on the lines below, write out your three biggest, boldest, fearless life goals that you would pursue assuming that you could use Other People's Money (OPM) to achieve them:

1. _____

2. _____

3. _____

OTHER PEOPLE'S MONEY

Often as a business owner, you will experience times when cash flow is hard to come by. In my business as an author and speaker, prior to getting a publishing deal done with John Wiley & Sons, Inc., I was a self-published author who always had to pay for my printing. On two different occasions over nine years, no matter how I looked at it, I did not have the cash to pay for books. Yet I had speaking engagements coming up where I could sell books to the audience. In both cases (years apart), I turned to close friends and business partners for help. First, it was Rick Frommer who paid for a print run, and he just said to pay him back whenever I could. No interest, no agreement, no promissory note, just "pay me back when you can." It took me about 18 months, and then he was paid back in full. A couple of years later, it was Taylor Clark who covered the costs of a large print run for me. No credit check required—he just sent me a check and asked to be paid back within a year. The full principal borrowed and then some was paid back in a year. I will be forever grateful for these two Angel Investors who just stepped up to the plate and offered some financial assistance to a fellow entrepreneur in need. For that reason, both of these friends and business partners will forever have their names etched in the "Acknowledgments" section of all of my books as I will never forget their acts of genuine assistance to an entrepreneur in need.

How many people do you know who believe so much in you and in your business that they are willing to become Angel Investors to support you in your dream as you build your business? Always reach out to these people and develop relationships; the world is full of Affluent Entrepreneurs eager to help other AEs in need.

EXERCISE

List five people you know, like, and trust who would be willing to step in and provide you with "Angel Investment" funds should you ever run into a jam in your business. When inserting the names below, it will also help you tremendously if these folks are already in the same industry as you since they will better understand the upside of your venture.

1. _____

2. _____

3. _____

4. _____

5. _____

Next, in addition to using Other People's Money (OPM) think about other areas where you can apply leverage for the growth of your business. How about:

Other People's Talent (OPT)

Other People's Knowledge (OPK)

Other People's Contacts (OPC)

Other People's Education (OPE)

You have heard the old saying that the difference in regards to grade point average is that all the A and B students end up working for the C students, while the C students are the ones who become successful entrepreneurs. The reason they (we) got Cs is because we were always playing sports, working a job (or two), or building a business while still taking a full course load. I am convinced that if I didn't have anything to do while in school but just school itself, then instead of getting Bs and Cs I could have gotten all As.

My point is that as an Affluent Entrepreneur, you need to find people more talented than you in every aspect of your business and then hire them to run that portion of your business. At some point, your business will be able to run on autopilot in your absence because of the talent assembled around you. This strategy is a real keeper for the Affluent Entrepreneur.

AFFLUENT ENTREPRENEUR PROFILE
LARRY PAGE AND SERGEY BRIN

Larry Page and Sergey Brin may not yet be household names, but they soon will be since the two Stanford Computer Science graduate students are the cofounders of Google. Google, Inc., has fast become one of the largest Internet companies in the world by using its search engine and online advertising strategies. Only a handful of companies I know of have been so successful that their company name has become a verb. Just look at how we refer to the process of searching for information on the Internet as "Googling" this or "Googling" that. To my knowledge, the only other companies that have turned their names into verbs are FedEx, with the phrase, "I am going to FedEx you a package," and Photoshop for when you "Photoshop a picture."

In 1998, Larry and Sergey had this fantastic vision of creating a newer, faster way to search for data on the Internet. Their only problem was that as graduate students, they didn't have the financial means to fund such an enterprise. One of their Stanford professors suggested they meet with the professor's friend who was an investor and computer guru. His name was Andy Bechtolsheim, and he had sold his company to Cisco Systems for hundreds of millions of dollars years earlier; he was also a cofounder of Sun Microsystems. Intrigued by what Larry and Sergey's professor had told him about their idea for a better and faster way to search the Internet, Bechtolsheim agreed to meet with the two of them.

As a result of this meeting, Bechtolsheim became their first investor when he wrote a check to "Google, Inc." for $100,000 on the spot. At the time, the company didn't even have a corporate bank account yet. A few weeks later, Google incorporated, and Larry and Sergey opened a bank account and deposited this "OPM" (Other People's Money) into its account. In the months to come, Larry and Sergey raised over $1 million to purchase the computer equipment needed to take their project to the next level. The rest is history. Today, virtually everyone on the Internet uses Google as the search engine of choice, and as a result, both Larry and Sergey have amassed a net worth close to $18 billion each. Not a bad return on using $1M in OPM to create their fortunes. More important than their fortunes is what they have created for all of us, a better way to search the Internet.

SUMMARY

Whether your business is just starting out or has been around for a while, if it is in need of cash flow to take it to the next level, I firmly believe that, when you can't get a loan at the bank, your line of credit is maxed out, and your personal savings are dried up, using OPM (Other People's Money) may be your best solution.

Try to find people you already like, know, and trust who are also in your industry as they will be more willing to invest in your venture. Also, do everything you can to negotiate favorable terms, while also doing all you can so that you do not relinquish or give up ownership in your business (however, at times this may not be possible). If you are forced to give up part of your business, make sure you keep the controlling interest at 51 percent or greater so you remain in control.

Do make good on your loan by cashing out your investors as soon as possible so they can enjoy their return on investment. Finally, by no means feel guilty or shy about asking for Angel Investors or venture capital to help you out. Chances are, the people from whom you are seeking investment funds, most likely were, in their early days, also in your shoes and had people who believed in them (their investors) who provided them the means to make their ventures fly.

If two graduate students can completely change the way we surf the Internet using OPM, then you too can use OPM to take your business to the next level and increase your companies' products or services in the marketplace. These sometimes hidden investors make the world go around and are responsible for the success of hundreds of thousands of businesses throughout the world. Before you run out of money, leverage OPM, and your business will soar! And while you are funding your business, don't forget to use OPT, OPK, OPC, and OPE if you want to grow your business even faster.

Prospecting 50 Percent of Your Working Hours

Only put off for tomorrow what you are
willing to die having left undone.
—Pablo Picasso

In this chapter, you will learn why your business cannot and will not grow unless you are looking for ways to drive revenue to your bottom line. Too many people have the mind-set of "Build it and they will come!" You'll learn that as CEO of your own company, you wear many hats, but your most important role is the VP of Sales. With the strategies offered in this chapter, you will see that no matter what challenges you face in business, your most important role is driving revenue to your bottom line.

To succeed in this role, you must understand that if you work an eight-hour day, then you must spend half of each and every day prospecting. If you don't like this activity, then you'll learn how to attract successful salespeople to your team who will prospect, prospect, and prospect. Prospecting is the most pivotal part of your business success. Finally, you will learn where J. Paul Getty's prospecting activities took him and how the results allowed him to become one of the wealthiest people alive in his time.

MANAGING YOUR TIME

Without question, the single greatest challenge all entrepreneurs have is managing their time appropriately. You are pulled in all directions, all of the time. As I sit writing this book, another call just came in from some knucklehead asking me for 15 minutes of my time to do some stupid interview or survey over the phone. Are you serious? This is the fifth time in as many days where I have gotten this call. My favorite part of the conversation is that even after I politely advise the caller that I am under a deadline and can't help him out, his next question is always, "Well, then, when would be a better time for us to call you back?" How about *never*! "Please," I ask kindly, "remove my name from your list."

The bottom line is that as an entrepreneur, we do everything and wear every hat, so how we spend our time is absolutely the most important part of our business. My friend and mentor Brian Tracy is a big fan of prospecting first thing in the morning. One time when we both spoke at the same seminar, on the car ride there, he gave me the following advice about prospecting and getting rejected. "If you want to make a million dollars per year, then do everything you can to get 10 smack down, in your face rejections by 9 AM each business day."

I agree with Brian; if you are continually prospecting, then you will make more money than you will know what to do with. Ten rejections are worth it if you get one "Yes." Even if you get 50 rejections in a day, one "Yes" may be all you need.

The challenge that remains as an entrepreneur is that you hold just about every position in your company, including:

President

Chief Executive Officer (CEO)

Chief Operating Officer (COO)

Chief Technology Officer (CTO)

Accountant

Accounts Payable Manager

Accounts Receivable Manager

Computer Guy

VP of Sales

Oh, and don't forget, you are also the Janitor. With all these roles tugging at you, the challenge becomes: How can you find time to prospect if you are stuck in your office doing administrative busy work all day?

THE 50 PERCENT RULE

Several years ago, one of my friends, Dennis Sutter, shared the 50 Percent Rule with me that he used to coach his clients. I have applied it to my business because it flat-out works! I also share it with all my clients to help them grow their revenues. Before he retired, Dennis was a real estate coach who helped real estate agents to double their income. He saw the problem that almost all business owners have—the more sales we make, the busier we get servicing our clients' ever-demanding needs, and in doing so, we inhibit our ability to continue prospecting for new clients.

Therefore, Dennis taught me to apply the 50 Percent Rule to my business. What this rule means is that no matter what you do, no matter what your time constraints are, no matter what deadlines you have, you must always spend a minimum of 50 percent of your time prospecting.

For example, if you are in the direct selling business and only have two hours per day to build your business because you have a full-time job, then you need to spend at least one of those two hours prospecting. Conversely, if you are full-time in your business and average working 10 hours per day, then you need to spend 5 hours per day prospecting for more clients.

Bottom line as the CEO of your company, if you are committed to become an Affluent Entrepreneur, you need to focus 50 percent of your working hours wearing your VP of Sales hat and driving new revenues to your business. If you don't like selling or prospecting, then you need to have deep pockets so you can hire a sales force to do it for you and accept that no one is going to be able to market your business as well as you can.

I know; you're thinking there is no way you can spend that much time prospecting. What is the solution if you can't apply the 50 Percent Rule to your business? You either need to accept the fact that you are going to become a struggling entrepreneur, or you need to delegate or outsource all the work you don't want to do.

OUTSOURCING

As we discussed earlier in the book, you need to look for virtual assistants, virtual business partners, and virtual salespeople to work in partnership with you to achieve your revenue goals. I have about 30 joint venture partners I work with all around the country to help me drive revenue to my business. I have a book-keeper who pays all my bills and an accountant who keeps me on the straight and narrow with the IRS. I have a computer guy, who also doubles as my web master to keep my presence on the Internet. I have a VP of Sales who is always hunting for big elephants. Oh yeah, and I have an amazing editor and proofreader who reviews all my copy before it is released.

As a result of outsourcing all of these important tasks I don't want to deal with in my business, I am freed up to do the three primary things I enjoy more than anything else: speak profession-ally, book more speaking engagements, and coach my clients on publishing their books and becoming best-selling authors.

EXERCISE

Think for a minute about your business and list below five roles you currently have in your business but don't enjoy:

1. _____

2. _____

3. _____

4. _____

5. _____

Now, list five people (whom you probably already know in your life) to whom you could contract or outsource this work:

1. _____

2. _____

3. _____

4. _____

5. _____

You may be hesitant to hire other people to help you because you're thinking, *How in the world am I going to be able to afford to hire these five people?* Well, first of all, you are not going to hire them as employees with salaries and benefits; you are going to outsource your undesirable work to them as independent contractors with no salary, only an hourly wage with a preset limit to the amount of hours required to perform the roles you ask them to perform.

For example, if you do the math, you may find out that it will cost you $2,000 per month to outsource this work. However, as a result of reappropriating all of these tasks, you'll have "found time" to prospect, which may bring you in an extra $10,000 per month in revenue, thus resulting in a net gain of $8,000. And that's a realistic and conservative example for a small business owner.

Maybe you are a bigger business so you will actually need to pay out $20,000 per month to free up your time. As a result, if you are hunting for big elephants, I suspect with this horsepower behind you, you could bring in $100,000 per month resulting in an $80,000 net profit. You get the point: Outsource and delegate to your team so it frees you up to prospect, prospect, prospect!

IF YOU BUILD IT, THEY WILL NOT COME

What do I mean by this phrase? Well, one my favorite movies from years ago, *Field of Dreams* starring Kevin Costner, was about an Iowa farmer who plowed over his crops to build a baseball field so some fictional baseball players would return from the dead and revive themselves to play baseball there each night. In the film, Kevin Costner's character keeps hearing this voice that tells him, "If you build it, they will come!" Finally, he decides to build the baseball field, and then the baseball players show up. Of course, this idea works in Hollywood movies (and it's a great movie by the way), but it does not work that way in the real world.

I remember 10 years ago, when I first self-published *Creating Your Own Destiny*, I called up Dan Poynter, who was and still is the self-publishing guru for all ages. I told him I had $500 left in my book budget and that I needed some coaching. He said, "For $500, I will give you two hours of my time." I quickly agreed, and it was one of the best investments I have ever made because I learned what I believe today to be one of the single greatest marketing secrets by which every Affluent Entrepreneur lives.

Dan Poynter taught me that a successful book is just like raising a successful child. He advised that a mother will gestate a child for nine months before giving birth. Conversely, it can take an author nine months of writing before publishing his book. Next, he said the mother (and hopefully father too) will then spend the next 18 to 22 years of her life raising the child. So just like raising kids, as an author you must spend the next 18 to 22 years raising your book if you are to be successful.

With this wisdom in mind, I have applied this metaphor to my business as an entrepreneur, and I share it with all my clients as well. The point is this: Just because you launch your business (open store front, start your online presence, manufacture your product, create your service, etc.), it doesn't mean you will be successful. Getting into business and launching a product or service is only 5 percent of the work. Just because you build the business, it doesn't mean the customers will come. Billions and billions of dollars could have been saved from waste if all business owners applied this knowledge to their lives.

Just as with creating a bestseller, 95 percent of the work is in the marketing and promoting of the book. Just like raising a successful, confident, contributing member of society, your child needs 95 percent of your effort to be raised correctly, so when you open your business, you must spend the rest of your life doing the 95 percent part in marketing if you are to be successful.

AFFLUENT ENTREPRENEUR PROFILE
J. PAUL GETTY

J. Paul Getty was many things in life, including an oil tycoon and a playboy. Throughout his life, he struggled with his marital relationships; he may not have been a moral role model, but when he worked and prospected for new opportunities, his work ethic was tireless and effective. After graduating from Oxford in 1914 with a degree in economics and political science, Getty spent his summers working his father's oil fields in Oklahoma. That was just the beginning.

In his autobiography titled, *How to Be Rich*, Getty wrote that the keys to success were to: (1) Rise early, (2) Work hard, and (3) Strike oil. Following this model eventually allowed him to gain controlling interest in over 200 companies including Getty Oil.

While others in the oil industry remained content to search for oil in the United States, Getty decided to learn Arabic and prospect on the other side of the world in the Middle East. He discovered a piece of land near the border of Saudi Arabia and Kuwait that he was convinced had oil and lots of it. As a result, he agreed to pay the

(continued)

(*continued*)

King of Saudi Arabia $1 million per year and $9.5 million in cash up front for the right to drill this land over the next 60 years. After four years and a $30 million investment, no oil had been discovered.

However, in 1953, Getty hit the jackpot, and his oil wells produced 16 million barrels per year for many, many years to come. This finding made him one of the wealthiest individuals on the planet with an estimated net worth eventually to exceed $1 billion.

SUMMARY

I never said that becoming an Affluent Entrepreneur would be easy. In fact, it will not. That is why there are no crowds at the top of the mountain. Most people are not willing to do what it takes to be successful. The Struggling Entrepreneur would not be willing to learn Arabic and travel to the ends of the earth to prospect the way J. Paul Getty did.

Always remember that the success of your business will not come with the building of your business, but rather with the marketing, prospecting, and customer acquisition duties you perform over the course of several years. "Overnight" success may take you 10 to 15 years.

Therefore, no matter how busy you get wearing a multitude of hats and playing numerous roles in your business, make sure that your VP of Sales hat is the one you most often wear. Spend 50 percent of your working hours prospecting. As a result, sales will be made, your revenue will come in, and you will be on your way to becoming an Affluent Entrepreneur!

Building Your Brand Identity

*If you would not be forgotten as soon as you are dead
and rotten, either write something worth reading,
or do things worth the writing.*
—Benjamin Franklin

With so many businesses in today's market, it's all about branding—standing out and identifying your business in a positively unforgettable way. So with this principle, you will learn how and why to build a unique brand for your business. You will learn about developing a successful web site, successful sales collateral items, and a sound business model. You will learn how to select a logo and color scheme for your company. You will learn what I believe to be the world's greatest marketing tool, and how to create that marketing tool for your business.

Furthermore, you will learn Seth Godin's wisdom on how to make your brand stand out from your competition. You will also learn why Ralph Lauren changed his birth name and built his entire company on remaining true to his brand, which is still going strong nearly 40 years later. Branding your business well will ultimately result in increased revenues and set you up to become an Affluent Entrepreneur.

The challenge we all have in business as entrepreneurs is that there is a good chance you and I are not the only ones in our markets offering our type of products and services. As a result, at times we can all get lost in the crowd of others doing what we do. Because of this overcrowding, if you do not do something to stand out, you may find yourself in a position where you aren't earning what you desire, or worse, find yourself struggling financially.

One of my all-time favorite mentors, thinkers, and marketers on this planet is a guy named Seth Godin who has written numerous books on sales, marketing, and leadership. My all-time favorite book of his is *Purple Cow*. Godin preaches that the key to success for a small business owner is to find a means to be different in a unique and attractive way so that his product will stand out from the crowd and be noticed. For example, let's say you look across a Midwest pasture and see hundreds of black and white cows. Then all of a sudden, you see a purple and white cow. You are certainly going to take notice and do your due diligence to learn more about this unique cow. The same is true with your business. You need to figure out how you are going to be different, unique, and most important, desirable to your clients.

An example of this purple cow strategy is a pricing model I used on my book *Creating Your Own Destiny*. After having sold over 100,000 copies, I kept getting e-mails from people advising me that they applied my book to their lives and their businesses and made an extra $1,000 last month or an extra $5,000. One woman even e-mailed me with excitement to tell me that one of the principles learned in *Creating Your Own Destiny* she applied to her business accounted for an extra $10,000 from a recent client.

These success stories made me start to question why in the world some of the best business, real estate, and entrepreneurship books are priced at only $19.95–$29.95 depending on page count and whether they are hardcover or softcover when the information included in these books, if applied correctly to your life, is worth virtually tens of thousands, if not hundreds of thousands of dollars. As a result of this thinking, and these e-mails from my readers, I decided to implement a new bold marketing strategy for my book. I decided I would implement it for a year and then measure the results.

See, the Affluent Entrepreneur is kind of like a scientist. We are constantly testing and measuring marketing campaigns and performing trial and error on sales offers. Some marketing and sales strategies work, some don't; so we adjust, move forward, and invest more time and money into those campaigns that work.

My idea was to be the first to test market the world's most valuable book *Creating Your Own Destiny* with a $1,000 price tag on the book. On the inside flap my pricing was listed as:

$1,000.00 US*

(*Includes two-hour consultation call with author. Without this option, book is $24.95 US)

Well, I tested and measured the results. My first thought was that I hadn't sold many books, so I returned my pricing back to $24.95. Sometime later I reevaluated this strategy and realized I had actually sold nearly 250 of these books combined with a publishing coaching package at a price point of $3,000–$4,000. Therefore, maybe I wasn't that far off my target. My point here, as Seth Godin says, is we need to be different in order to get noticed.

EXERCISE

List five things you can implement in your business ASAP so you will be different, stand out, and get noticed by your prospects:

1. _____

   _____

   _____

2. _____

   _____

   _____

3. _____

   _____

   _____

4. _____

   _____

   _____

5. _____

   _____

   _____

Pricing, as in the example above, is one of my favorite aspects in the concept of branding. Why? Because the error that Struggling Entrepreneurs make but Affluent Entrepreneurs laugh at has to do with pricing the actual product or service. See, the Struggling Entrepreneur believes that whoever has the lowest price wins. The Affluent Entrepreneur knows that price is one of the last things to consider when marketing your services.

For example, whenever I travel, I often stop at the burrito shop at Sea-Tac airport and order a chicken quesadilla. I always ask for extra meat and extra cheese because flying anywhere from Seattle is a long flight, and I don't want to be stuck on a plane being hungry. I am always entertained when whoever is behind the counter tells me they can't give me extra chicken and extra cheese because it would cost me an extra dollar. They always assume I don't have an extra dollar in my pocket so I am going to go hungry on my flight. I always respond and say, "I don't care if it costs an extra five dollars; give me extra chicken and cheese."

See, the scarcity mind-set will not serve you as a business owner. As Affluent Entrepreneurs, we must always assume that our prospects have money in their pockets and bank accounts, and are willing to pay more for the extra value we provide with our brand.

This example reminds me of one of my all-time favorite speakers and mentors in the world. Zig Ziglar says, "There is a difference between price and cost." What he means is that often, higher-priced items actually cost less than lower priced ones in the long run because lower-priced items always seem to break down and fall apart sooner, requiring us to repurchase before we would have, had we invested in the higher-priced items from the get go.

Another piece of Zig's wisdom I have always found amusing is when he talks about authors selling their books after their speeches. Zig says that authors need to develop the following mind-set, "I have your books; you have my money . . . I am here to make the switch!"

BRANDING "YOU"

As the Affluent Entrepreneur, you are the brand your customers want. They want your signature, your imprint, your branding. They want you! That is why people prefer Ralph Lauren's Polo brand jeans compared to Wal-Mart's Faded Glory brand. People always want a Mercedes Benz or BMW over a Hyundai or Chevrolet. It all comes down to branding.

So the question is this: How can you brand yourself, your products, or services? People often ask, "What if I have a job and work for a major Fortune 500 company? Can I brand myself as an employee?" Absolutely you can. Not only can you, but you must if you are to protect yourself from layoffs and downsizing.

As an employee you must show up to work every day, putting forth your best effort, continuing to build your brand yourself as one of the most valuable employees in the organization. You must look at yourself as an entrepreneur, with your number one customer being your employer. Your employer is your top priority. Whatever need, goal, or objective your employer has set out for you to accomplish, not only must you meet that goal, but you also should go the extra mile to outperform the other employees.

In doing so, the results you create will give you the confidence and resume to go out and get another job should you be served with layoff papers. Or better yet, you will gain the confidence to go out and start your own business and become an Affluent Entrepreneur.

So how can you, as an Affluent Entrepreneur, brand yourself? Here is a listing of the best ways in which you can brand yourself:

1. Have your photo on your business card, web site, book, and auto-signature in e-mail.

2. Use a consistent color scheme on all of your marketing materials.

3. Create "branding statements" that capture your prospects' attention.

4. Create a "branding name" that is unforgettable and that the media will use to refer to you.

5. Create "branding web sites" that speak exactly to your product or service.

6. Have your signature on all of your work, web site, book, and so on. . . .

Let's look at each of these items individually to see how you can incorporate these suggestions into your business:

First, go out and get a world-class photo taken by a professional in your nicest suit and tie. If you don't like the way it looks, have the professional Photoshop it to make you look your very best. My photo was taken when I just returned from a family vacation in Maui so I was super tan. Rarely am I that tan. Also, I had a couple of fever blisters on my lips due to the sunburn, which the experts were able to Photoshop away.

Second, my color scheme for my business includes the following colors: blue, beige, teal, and gold. I use these four colors over and over again in all I do with my books, web site, flyers, and business cards. You can do the same. Find a color scheme that matches your passion, your message, and your business model, and then stay consistent.

Third, create a branding statement on your site to gain your prospects' attention. On my main web site, www.PatrickSnow .com, I have a couple of different branding statements at the top to attract visitors. These include:

"Helping You Get More Out of Life and Work . . ."

I don't know about you, but I certainly want more out of life and work. Virtually everyone wants *more* out of life, and I believe that when we create and follow our own destinies, we can get more out of life! The next one is on my publishing site:

"Helping Entrepreneurs Become Best-Selling Authors . . ."

Again, if you are going to write a book, don't you want to become a best-selling author? Let's face it; there is no reason to play unless you are going to play to win. These are two examples of "branding statements" that I use in my business. Now, get creative and make your own branding statements. In the exercise below, go ahead and create your own "branding statements." However, be sure that you use the word "you" so you are talking directly to your prospects. A second strategy is to speak to your prospects' niche, which is not as good as saying "you" but better than missing out altogether.

EXERCISE

Write out two branding statements below (one using the word "you" in it and the other identifying prospects by their niche):

1. _____

   _____

   _____

2. _____

   _____

   _____

Fourth, create a "branding name" for yourself that will make people remember you. Since we talked about Seth Godin earlier in this chapter, it is important to note that he is called "America's Greatest Marketer." Who wouldn't want to be called that? I don't know if he gave himself that label, or someone else gave it to him, but it doesn't matter—either way, that branding is genius.

When I first started my speaking business in the early 1990s, another professional in the industry asked me, "Well after all, just who is Patrick Snow, and why should we care?" I realized at the time there was a point to that question. Since I was just starting to think about writing a book about "destiny," I figured I needed to brand myself using the word "destiny" and the "study" or "teacher of destiny." Having recently graduated from the University of Montana, academic titles were in my thoughts, so I called up my web master, Tony Wall, and told him to call me, "Patrick Snow, 'The Dean of Destiny.'" He did just that, and I have included it in all of my speaking introductions ever since. It has stuck and now people regularly refer to me as "The Dean of Destiny."

You can do the same. Think for a moment, right now, about what your "branding name" can be. Once you have nailed it, use it on your web site, and all of your other marketing materials.

Fifth, create "branding web sites" that speak to your product or service. I have about 50 web sites that all strategically point to different locations, and each has search engine optimization (SEO) to the others. Below is a list of some of my sites. Ask yourself as you read these names, whether you can tell what the purpose, mission, or goal of each site is:

www.CreatingYourOwnDestiny.com

www.TheAffluentEntrepreneur.com

www.BestSellerPublishingCoaching.com

www.BestSellerBookCoaching.com

www.HawaiiTigerSharks.com

www.TheDeanofDestiny.com

www.OutEarnYourBills.com

www.PatrickSnow.com

You get the point. Make sure that you capitalize the first letter of each word in your domain names so that you make it easier for your prospects to read and memorize them. Just by reading these links, you can tell, for the most part, exactly what the purpose of each of these sites is. I encourage you to do the same. Purchasing a web site is similar to buying waterfront property to build on at a later time. Web sites, often referred to as URLs, are in limited quantity, so secure a dozen or more for you and your family to build on whenever you feel the time is right. You never know; perhaps if you don't purchase the web site name you want, someone else might purchase it first and not even use it but simply be "squatting," a term used in the industry for people who purchase domain names just so they can resell them later at a higher price. Someone recently sold www.Pizza.com for $1 million. You get the point. Buy now; build later when you're ready.

Finally, place your "signature" on all of your work. When I published the first edition of *Creating Your Own Destiny* in 2001, I asked Dan Poynter whether or not I should sign my books. He replied, "Always sign your books. They are more valuable with your signature on them than if not." I guess that makes sense. Let me ask you: Would you rather have a Babe Ruth rookie baseball card, or that same card with his signature on it? Of course, the signature always makes the item more valuable.

For that reason, I have included my "Patrick Snow" signature on the top portion of each and every page on my web site. You should do the same. Always, sign your letters and include your signature on all of your marketing pieces. Doing so will enhance your brand.

I am always amazed that people will wait in line after I speak to have me sign their books or sign their notes. If they only knew that I am just an ordinary guy aspiring to live an extraordinary life, perhaps they wouldn't wait in line. However, one thing I have learned is that when you write a book, people look at you in a whole new way and treat you as if you were a celebrity, professional athlete, or famous musician.

Now take a look at this list of six items I've provided you, all of which you can do immediately with all of your marketing pieces so they will better brand you and your product or service. You may also want to consider putting your brand on hats, T-shirts, bumper stickers, and so on.

However, none of these strategies above will work as well as my final recommendation for your business. There is one marketing and branding strategy above all others that will help promote, grow, and brand your business better than the rest. This strategy once implemented will become hands down the absolutely greatest way to build your brand better than all the others. What is this secret? It is something that is considered to be one of the most highly respected careers in the world.

The Affluent Entrepreneur's best kept secret: You should publish a book to promote your business. No other marketing strategy will provide such a high level of return or branding on your investments. If this statement has attracted your interest, I encourage you to read my book:

Becoming a Best-Selling Author:

How to Use Your Book as a Lead-Generating Tool to Attract More Speaking, Coaching, and Consulting Opportunities

Let's face it; everyone you and I know is an expert at whatever it is he or she is most passionate about. My two teenage sons buy and sell Nike SB sneakers on the Internet and make quite a bit of extra money doing so. As a result, they are "experts" in the rare Nike SB sneaker business, and the inside term for the customers buying all of these shoes from my sons is "sneakerheads." It is a huge business, and my two sons have figured it out and are now profiting off this trend. However, since they don't have the term "author" next to their names on their business cards (in fact they don't even have business cards), no one in the media will acknowledge either of them as the "expert."

Here are the reasons why you need to write a book:

1. To give away to your prospects as a sampling of your business.

2. To impact the lives of those who read your book.

3. To boost your credentials to earn higher fees in your business.

4. To get free publicity with media.

I am convinced that after speaking in this industry since I was 17 years old, I have learned that there is no greater marketing tool, or branding secret than writing a book. I am so passionate about this subject that I have spent the last 10 years of my life when I have not been on the road speaking, at home coaching other entrepreneurs to write and publish their books. If you see the value in this branding strategy to grow your business and are interested in publishing a book, I would be thrilled to offer you a complimentary phone consultation. First, go ahead and read every word and listen to the audio on the following site:

www.BestSellerBookCoaching.com

Then call or e-mail me to schedule your session. Oh, and by the way, I love all of the social networking sites out there; what I don't like is trying to remember all the darn user names and passwords required to use these tools. Therefore, I prefer you just e-mail me directly at Patrick@PatrickSnow.com.

AFFLUENT ENTREPRENEUR PROFILE
RALPH LAUREN

Ralph Lauren was born in the Bronx, New York, to immigrant parents from Belarus. His birth name was "Ralph Reuben Lifshitz." As a young boy, he decided

(continued)

(*continued*)

he would become a millionaire and told others of this goal. His brother changed their family name from "Lifshitz" to "Lauren," and it was a good thing since there is no way that the Polo brand could have stood the test of time with a name like "Lifshitz."

In high school, Ralph Lauren developed an eye for fashion and often sold ties to his classmates. He went off to college, dropped out, and did a stint in the army before he eventually landed a sales job with Brooks Brothers. In 1967, he opened his first store and launched his company Ralph Lauren, and in 1972, he created the now famous Polo emblem logo. He first launched this emblem on 24 colors of shirts that are now the brand of the entire industry since a "polo shirt" has come to mean any short-sleeve shirt with three buttons and a collar.

This iconic logo of the polo player on a horse has now been virtually unchanged since its original release nearly 40 years ago. The brand is recognized around the world as a clothing line of high fashion and solid quality, and as a symbol of wealth.

By staying true to its brand and not changing its emblem, Polo Ralph Lauren has 35 boutiques of its own, and its brand clothing is sold in high-end department stores across the world. Due to this successful branding strategy, the company went public in 1997, and in 2009 it had nearly $5 billion in revenue. After spending a lifetime building this single brand, Ralph Lauren has amassed a net worth estimated by *Forbes Magazine* to be at $4.6 billion.

SUMMARY

Building a world-class brand is not something you do overnight. It is something that takes a lifetime commitment to quality. It takes "purple cow" thinking—a willingness and the creativity to be different and to stick out from the crowd in order to be noticed.

Creating the brand is something you can do in a very short time, but marketing the brand will take a lifetime. There are numerous things you need to consider, such as your logo, your colors, your signature, and in Ralph Lauren's case, both his name change and his emblem.

Most important, in order to brand yourself, you must stay consistent and not change your brand on a whim; you must stay firm and spend the rest of your life marketing your brand. If you don't have the fashion sense Ralph Lauren has, or the marketing talent displayed by Seth Godin, then I suggest you consider writing a book because no other tool in the marketplace will help you build your credibility, strengthen your credentials, attract new clients, or impact your brand the way a hardcover book will.

Create your brand, and then stay strong, remain firm, and commit to spending a lifetime promoting your brand, and you will become an Affluent Entrepreneur quicker than you may expect.

PRINCIPLE 16

Hunting for Big Deals

Diamonds are nothing more than chunks
of coal that stuck to their jobs.
—Malcolm Forbes

I n this chapter, you will learn that it takes the same amount of
preparation, time, skill, and persistence to sell one widget as it
does to sell 10,000 widgets. You will learn why it doesn't make
sense to do business one at a time when, for the same effort, you can
market your business in volume and continuously push the enve-
lope as you explore what's possible. You'll gain the confidence
needed to start at the top when calling on buyers and work your
way down the ladder, instead of starting at the bottom and fighting
your way to the top. You will learn how to hunt for "big elephant"
prospects and get into the mind of perhaps the biggest elephant
investor of our time, Mr. Warren Buffett.

Several years ago, I learned that working for just an hourly
wage is to accomplish nothing other than to trade your most prized
possession, your time, for money. Talk about a waste of time. As
a young boy, I quickly learned that I could go off and get a job and
be paid $3.35 per hour (minimum wage at the time), or I could
sell my products or services and work a whole lot less and make a
whole lot more.

When I was a sophomore in high school, I took a job flipping
burgers at a local hangout called Country Ranch. This burger
place served the best burgers and frozen cokes around. However,
after I figured out the amount of time I was putting in to make
only $3.35 per hour, I soon realized there had to be a better way.
That better way was to get into sales.

In the winters of my earlier days, I would go door to door with my shovel in hand and sell homeowners on believing that my back was strong enough to shovel their driveways and my time was worth about $20. Most of these jobs took me about 30 to 45 minutes, and then I would go back up to the house, ring the door bell, and retrieve my $20 bill. I remember one huge storm we had in Michigan that winter where I did this all day long, and I made $200 in a day. Now for a 12-year-old kid, that is a lot of money. I remember taking this money and going down to the electronics store and purchasing my first boom box, complete with detachable speakers and a cassette player. . . . Wow, it didn't get any better than that.

During the summers, I would do the exact same thing, except instead of a shovel, my father let me borrow the family lawnmower (of course, only after our own lawn was mowed). I would then go throughout the neighborhood pushing our family mower while looking for homes with tall grass. I would do this anytime during the summer when I was bored, usually whenever I couldn't find any of the neighbor kids to play wiffle ball or home run derby. The life of being a kid—how I sometimes miss the simplicity of that lifestyle: my only concerns were what's for dinner, what time do I have to go to bed, and do those cute girls in my class like me as much as I like them. A pretty good life I must say.

Looking back at my youth and applying those lessons to my adult life of becoming an entrepreneur, the biggest "Aha!" moment I have had is that at a young age, I learned you could make far more money in sales than you can as an employee trading time for dollars. Not only that, but you become your own boss, set your own calendar, work whenever you are not playing wiffle ball, and have a much better life.

The lessons served me well because as soon as I graduated from college, I entered the sales field, selling corporate travel against other travel agencies. Next, I sold overnight air express against other delivery companies. Finally in my last sales career, I sold printed circuit boards against other circuit board manufacturers.

During those years, I had a huge awakening: As long as I left it up to someone else to manufacture the product (circuit boards) or perform the service (overnight air express), as the salesperson I could not control the finished and final experience for my customers. This final product or service was always left in the hands of other people. As a result, I can't tell you how many times while working in the air express business I had to call my contact and apologize for their payroll not showing up (this was before the days of direct deposit) due to an "Act of God," which was usually just a snowstorm at the main hub in Ohio where hundreds of planes would fly each night, sort all the freight, and then return the next day with all of the packages. Also, I often would end up taking calls from Intel (my biggest client), explaining to them why their circuit boards would not be delivered on time, thereby causing them to miss their build schedule.

These continued headaches over the years led me to have two epiphanies: (1) If I were going to maximize my wealth and true earning abilities, then I needed to pursue a career in sales; and (2) I needed to be the one who creates the product or performs the services so I can be in complete control of the results my customer wants. As a result, I no longer sell for anyone else. What I do today is market my services as a professional keynote speaker, and as a book publishing, book marketing, and speaking coach. Additionally, I market copies of my book in large volumes throughout the world.

As a result of pursuing this model, I am the only one in complete control of the product or service that my clients experience. I am in control of my destiny, I am in control of my earning limits (or no limits), and I am the one ultimately in control of providing for my family. This last sentence is especially important to me because when I was laid off at 9/11 and again in 2002, I was left feeling I had no control over the situation.

The most important principle you as a future Affluent Entrepreneur can take away from hearing my story is that you too must create your own product or service so that you can be in complete control of your customers' level of satisfaction and your full income potential.

EXERCISE

List five products or services you can create that you can bring to the marketplace.

1. _____

2. _____

3. _____

4. _____

5. _____

SELLING IN VOLUME

There is an old Native American tale where a grandfather and his grandson are standing atop a plateau looking down into the valley below and admiring all of the buffalo grazing. With excitement, the boy says to his grandfather, "Let's run down there and get us one of those buffalo." The grandfather replies to his grandson, "No. Let's walk down there and get them all."

This story illustrates what I'm talking about when I say "hunting for big elephants." Instead of looking to sell just one of your products or services, I am asking you to think outside of the box, expand your level of thinking, and sell large volumes of your products or services to single buyers.

Easier said than done. I know—I feel your pain. However, two books that I highly encourage you to read that will further drive home this point are *Strategic Selling* and *Conceptual Selling*, both by coauthors Robert Miller and Stephen Heiman, since both books will help you to understand the importance of always starting at the top. Find the individual who has the ability to authorize the check, sign the purchase order, or move forward with the sale.

Let me tell you about two of the biggest sales I have made in my career. The first was selling 40,000 copies of my first book, *Creating Your Own Destiny*, to a network marketing company. The second was actually selling the rights of my first book to the world's number one business publisher, John Wiley & Sons, Inc.

Let's start with the first example. In reading Dan Poynter's book, *The Self-Publishing Manual*, I learned that the commonly accepted number of books that needed to be sold in order for a book to be considered a bestseller was 35,000 copies. As a result, I set my sights on achieving this number ASAP. I found and interviewed book brokers who had relationships with direct selling companies that bought books by the tens of thousands for their Book-of-the-Month programs. As soon as I learned about this opportunity, I bet I sent in 20 sample preview copies of the book, let them know I could be flexible and work within their budget, and finally advised my front-line representative that I would authorize whatever she said it would take to make the deal happen.

When I said all this, I fully understood that many in the book selling business believe you should never accept less than $1 per book in net profit. Well, that was their model, not mine. I told my book broker I would do whatever it took to sell this volume and move 40,000 copies of my book as fast as I could. I was eager to make this sale happen and become an overnight bestseller. Well, long story short, word came back from my broker that after printing, shipping, and distribution, I would only earn 25 cents per book, or approximately $6,000. I immediately thought, *Literally, I have less than 30 minutes into this project so why not sign off on the deal.*

The so-called experts in the book marketing business advised me not to do the deal, but I went against their opinion and did the deal anyway. Later I learned that if I hadn't done the deal, three other authors were behind me, all ready to pull the trigger on their books. So I did the deal, and within four months of self-publishing my book, it was a best-seller. This deal and the prestige that went with having a best-selling book allowed me to increase my speaking, coaching, and consulting fees right from the get-go. The rest is history—it was that deal that gave me the confidence to pursue this business eventually on a full-time basis.

The next rule of thumb that you as the Affluent Entrepreneur must apply to your business is always to start at the top; when doing this, often the top person will make the introductions on lower levels to allow for the large "elephant" deals to go through.

Therefore, after selling an estimated 150,000 books in five languages over nine plus years, I realized that I had pretty much exhausted all of my resources in my quest to sell one million books and that if I were to achieve that goal, I needed to partner with one of the world's biggest publishers, John Wiley & Sons, Inc., the elephant of the business book publishing industry. My research found that Wiley was roughly 200 years old and did something like $3 billion per year in sales. Additionally, it is the number one business publisher in the world, owning about 15 percent of the business book market. From the get-go, it was my goal to land a publishing deal with this phenomenal company.

Therefore, after several unsuccessful attempts using literary agents, I learned that, according to the Publishers Marketing Association (PMA), only 80 percent of book deals are done directly with literary agents. To me, that meant that 20 percent of book publishing deals were done directly with publishing companies without using an agent, thereby allowing the author to save 15 percent on royalties and 15 percent on the advance. Obviously, I decided going solo was the way to attract a publisher's attention.

My next step in the process was watching a video on www .DailySuccessStream.com and listening to Mark Victor Hansen summarize how he attended BookExpo America and went booth to booth handing out review copies of his book. I figured that I could do the exact same thing. This process reminds me of the anonymous quote, "If you want what others have, do what they did, and you will get what they got!"

I followed Mark Victor Hansen's lead. I booked a speaking engagement in Manhattan, where the next BookExpo America was being held. Then I reserved a hotel room, secured my airline ticket, and I was in business. Six weeks later, I landed at New York's La Guardia airport, went into Manhattan, and checked into my hotel room. Once checked in, I went over to scout the floor layout of the Jacob Javits Convention Center to determine where Wiley's booth was located. I also took note of several of the other major publishers, all of which seemed to be in the same general area.

I returned to my hotel room, put on my suit and tie, and proceeded to go deliver my speech that night. Case in point, whenever I travel, I always attempt to deliver a speech while on a trip so I can make the trip (or at least a portion of it) tax deductible. As an Affluent Entrepreneur, you must also combine business with leisure if you are to minimize your tax burden and maximize your business.

I woke up early the next morning and took a cab over to the Jacob Javits Convention Center after a pit stop at the post office to pick up boxes of my book. I arrived and rented out space on the lower level reserved for luggage and such. I used this space as home base and left my boxes of books there. I put 20 hard copies in a shoulder bag and went booth to booth handing out copies to key representatives (typically acquisition editors) of major publishers. I was surprised at how many twenty-somethings right out of college advised me that I couldn't hand out books on the exhibit floor. I thought to myself, *This is what they are trained to do, but I am not going to let someone else's stick-to-the-rules mentality stop me from accomplishing my mission.*

After 60 minutes or so of handing out books to acquisition editors and networking with others in attendance, I stopped at the John Wiley & Sons, Inc. booth, which must have been bigger than my house. I bet their booth was 4,000 to 5,000 square feet and had 20 to 30 representatives from Wiley available and eager to help or answer questions.

I scanned the booth looking for the oldest, baldest (and I write this with no disrespect), wisest representative. I found my man; he was probably in his late fifties or maybe early sixties, and his name badge read Senior VP of Sales. I gave him a copy of my self-published hardcover *Creating Your Own Destiny*, and I advised him that I had been on the cover of *USA TODAY* and had sold more than 150,000 copies over nine years. I also told him I had a speaking engagement in Kuala Lumpur, Malaysia, later that fall, and I had no idea how I was going to get 500 copies of my book into Malaysia through customs. I finally advised him that after all these years, I was ready to partner with a world-class organization that could help me better achieve my book-marketing goals.

He looked me in the eye, shook my hand, and gave me his business card as I gave him three copies of my book. And he told me to come back in 60 minutes when the VP of Acquisitions would be available to meet with me. I was thrilled, tried to contain my enthusiasm, and left the booth. I must tell you that those 60 minutes seemed like they took forever.

When I came back 60 minutes later, the VP of Acquisitions asked me to step outside into the hallway so we could talk. Once in the hallway, he asked me whether the process of selling 150,000 books was easy or not. I could not tell where he was going with this or why he asked the question.

I responded with the honest-to-God truth and advised him that it was the most difficult thing career-wise I had ever done. I advised him that I had risked everything for this pursuit of my business except my faith and my family. I risked my perfect credit score, my house, everything. He said, "Good," and then advised that had I answered any other way, he would have questioned my genuineness.

He looked me in the eye and then said, "Yes, I think we can do a deal with you. I will send you a sample blueprint of a book proposal for you to use as a guideline. Complete the proposal, send it back, and we will make something happen." I asked him, "How much time do I have to complete the proposal?" thinking he would say a month or so. His answer was, "How about the end of the week?"

I gulped and thought, *Okay, he means business.* I flew home and on Monday morning started my proposal. I spent 14 hours writing, rewriting, and editing my proposal to turn it in two days later on that Wednesday. That was during the summer of 2009, and during that summer, Wiley did a two-book deal with me on my first book, *Creating Your Own Destiny,* and my second book, the book you are now reading, *The Affluent Entrepreneur.*

I share this detailed story with you for one reason and one reason only. John Wiley & Sons, Inc., is a $3 billion per year company that is over 200 years old. It is a big elephant, and I am encouraging you to pursue sales with big elephants. What are, and/or who are, the biggest prospects in your industry that you can pursue and land so that in doing so, you will become an Affluent Entrepreneur?

EXERCISE

List five of your largest "big elephant" prospects that you are pursuing:

1. _____

2. _____

3. _____

4. _____

5. _____

Now list five actions that you need to take ASAP to help these prospects get closer to purchasing your product or service:

1. _____
_____
_____

2. _____
_____
_____

3. _____

   _____

   _____

4. _____

   _____

   _____

   _____

5. _____

   _____

   _____

AFFLUENT ENTREPRENEUR PROFILE
WARREN BUFFETT

Warren Buffett is known to many in his hometown of Omaha, Nebraska, as the "Oracle of Omaha." Being a math genius in his childhood led him to a career in the investment business. From 1970 onward, he has served as Chairman and CEO of his own firm, Berkshire Hathaway Inc. After being an understudy of Benjamin Graham, Buffett developed his own style of hunting the marketplace for stocks trading at discounts to their true worth.

During the 1990s, Buffett avoided technology stocks altogether, and he readily admits that these companies are often beyond his comprehension. Instead, he has made billions sticking to companies he knows, organizations like Coca-Cola where his company owns $9.7 billion worth of Coke stock.

Buffett's investment rules are solid, and his track record from 1980 to 2006 is unbelievably amazing. If you had given Buffett $1,000 of your money to invest in the mid-1950s, he could have made you over $25 million by 2005.

Buffett's rules for investing are as follows. Rule number one: Don't lose money. Rule number two: Always remember rule number one. He too hunts for big elephants, and he advises, "When you bet, you must best big. Don't swing at a lot of pitches, but if you do swing, swing for the fences."

As a result of his abilities and a knack for crunching numbers, he has amassed a personal net worth of $47 billion. His company, Berkshire Hathaway, has become the eighteenth-largest corporation in the world as measured by market capitalization. In 2006, Buffett announced that he was going to give away 85 percent of his company's holdings to numerous foundations, with the Bill and Melinda Gates Foundation being one of the biggest recipients.

Summary

If you want to become an Affluent Entrepreneur, you must think like one and not focus on selling your products one at a time, but develop a big elephant mentality and sell in volume. Identify the biggest buyer of your products or services in your marketplace and be bold and go after that big elephant prospect. Remember the grandfather talking to his grandson who said, "How about we walk down there and get them all?" That is the kind of mentality you need to develop if you are to become an Affluent Entrepreneur.

Buffett's rules are never to lose money, to bet big, and not to swing all that often, but when you do swing, swing for the fences. The material in this chapter may be the most important in this book because by considering the ratio of the client to its wealth potential, you can determine whether an opportunity is a big elephant worth pursuing. Always remember, that big elephants will feed a lot of people for a long time, so I challenge you to pursue those big elephant prospects and you will be on your way to achieving your personal wealth goals.

Investing in Yourself

It is not the mountain that we conquer, but ourselves.
—Sir Edmund Hillary

In this chapter, you will learn the true difference between enter-tainment and education. You will learn why many people fail to create wealth and how to avoid the things in our lives that steal precious time and inhibit our ability to invest in ourselves. I will introduce you to a new online goal management system that is sure to reduce the time it takes you to achieve your goals. Finally, you will learn how the wealthiest American ever, John D. Rockefeller, made his fortune.

The challenge with many people today is that they believe their education is completed when they graduate from college. The reality is that education is a lifetime process. A famous anonymous quote sums it up:

> You will be the same person you are today in five years, except for the people you meet and the books you read.

I recently read an alarming statistic that said something like 60 percent of college graduates will never again read a book start to finish for the rest of their lives. If that is true, it is a sad statistic. I believe it is partly true today because of all the other choices competing for our time and our entertainment desires.

ENTERTAINMENT VERSUS EDUCATION

My good friend, best-selling author, and mentor Brian Tracy taught me the most about investing in yourself. Brian says that on average most people will spend only 1 hour investing in themselves for every 40 hours they spend entertaining themselves. If this ratio is even half true, it shows what we set as our priorities are not always in our best interests.

The challenge is that we are bombarded by entertainment options that include:

- Surfing the Internet

- Watching television

- Going to the movies

- Playing video games

- Attending athletic games

Not that there is anything wrong with enjoying these activities; the problem is that we can stunt our mental, emotional, and financial growth if we are focused on constantly creating the next "entertainment high." What Brian Tracy believes we must do and has spent much of his life preaching is that we need to take 100 percent responsibility for our lives. If something is in our lives that we don't like, we must take action to change it. So how do we change the things we don't like?

How about educating ourselves with new information and applying new knowledge to old problems to achieve new, exciting, and fulfilling results. Bottom line, we need to educate ourselves more and entertain ourselves less. Better yet, when we have a goal to achieve, a passion to do what we love, we will find ourselves entertained by the process of educating ourselves. So what are some ways we can change this ratio? How about instead of one hour of education for every 40 hours of entertainment, we spend 10 hours educating ourselves. In other words, apply the 4:1 ratio to your life.

Imagine how your life would change for the better if you spent 10 hours per week learning new skills, new strategies, new techniques, and new formulas to achieve your goals. Here are just a few examples of additional ways we can educate ourselves:

- Reading books
- Doing research on the Internet
- Listening to audio books/CDs in the car
- Attending seminars
- Making e-learning a part of our regimen
- Watching educational videos

FORMAL EDUCATION VERSUS SELF-EDUCATION

The famous author and philosopher Jim Rohn dedicated his entire life to preaching his message that formal education will make you a living, but self-education will make you a fortune. What he meant was that it is quite important to gain a solid formal education (high school, college, graduate school), but often, getting these degrees will not teach you how to create wealth. Sure, they will position you so that you may be qualified enough to be hired as an employee. However, I don't know a single person who ever achieved wealth solely by being an employee.

The Affluent Entrepreneur has come to learn the hard way that one of the best means for achieving wealth is to own your own business and become the employer. That is exactly what Jim Rohn is talking about. It is self-education through books, seminars, CDs, and studying other successful entrepreneurs that will give you the confidence, resources, knowledge, and know-how to achieve real wealth and create a fortune in your lifetime.

So while formal education is very important, it is not as important as self-education. Look at Bill Gates, one of the wealthiest individuals in the world. When he started Microsoft, he was a college dropout, but through his self-education, vision, and entrepreneurial pursuits, he has created a net worth in excess of

$53 billion. As a result of his entrepreneurial track records, he has also been awarded several honorary degrees.

WEALTH AND TAXES

One of the wisest financial gurus on the planet is a former IRS tax attorney by the name of Sandy Botkin, founder of the Tax Reduction Institute. He has studied wealth and taxes more than probably anyone else on the planet. He believes there are two primary reasons why so many people never achieve true wealth in their lives or in their businesses:

1. Failure to save 10 percent of their income

2. Overpaying their taxes

First, many of us are guilty of not saving. We constantly use 100 percent of our income to pay our bills, but ultimately, we never save for that rainy day. Sandy preaches that every time you get a paycheck, no matter how large or small and no matter what your circumstances, you must take 10 percent of it and save/invest in your future not in your bills.

Second, the IRS tax code has gotten so complex that if you don't have a tax professional who knows what she is doing, then no doubt, you are overpaying your taxes and not accurately taking advantage of all the deductions rightly due to you.

One of the best reasons to become a business owner is that business owners have numerous tax advantages, write-offs, and deductions that employees are never able to access or enjoy. Affluent Entrepreneurs have learned how to apply these tax advantages to their businesses so they never again overpay taxes and underpay their bank accounts. I highly recommend you visit Mr. Botkin's web site, www.TaxReductionInstitute.com, and apply his knowledge and resources to your life and your business. As a result, you will be back in control of how much money you give away in taxes.

TAKING CHARGE OF YOUR FUTURE

I firmly believe we all have the ability to predetermine our future and get exactly what we want out of life simply by creating a vision for how we want our lives to be, writing out these visions in the form of goals, taking actions on these goals, and achieving our destinies. This whole process is what my first book *Creating Your Own Destiny* is all about.

However, the more I travel the world speaking, the more I hear the same things over and over again. Basically, I hear every excuse possible for why people are not achieving their goals and dreams, but they usually come back to the same issue: goal setting. For whatever reason, most people lack the ability to write down their goals to create a road map or a game plan for their lives.

I encourage you to visit www.PatrickSnow.com and click on "Free Stuff." Once you do so, you can download the free goal sheet, which will guide you as you invest in yourself, your future, and your destiny. These goals sheets include:

- Life Plan Goal Sheet

- Balanced Living Goal

- Monthly Goal Sheet

- Many other special reports designed to help you invest in yourself

A BETTER WAY TO SET AND ACHIEVE YOUR GOALS

For those of you who like to do everything online and keep a permanent record of all of your goals, I would like to introduce you to a company that is forever changing the landscape of how we set and achieve our goals. Mindbloom is a company whose technology is rather mind-blowing.

What is Mindbloom? It is a social game that inspires real-life change. Created by award-winning graphic designers and game developers, it offers a fun, simple, and rewarding way to grow a healthy, balanced, and meaningful life with family and friends via the Web, Facebook, and mobile devices.

How does Mindbloom work? Mindbloom community members access the application online either from www.mindbloom .com, www.facebook.com, or one of Mindbloom's sponsored sites. New users select the three most important branches in life for them and after a couple of quick steps, the user's Life Tree is created for them. Users are encouraged to invite family and friends to enjoy the experience, building a community almost from the very first commitment they make.

The user's Life Tree evolves naturally—based on what is important at any given moment, and upon the unique areas, intentions, and actions that are most desired or highest priorities for the individual user. Users can also add images from their own photo libraries, enhancing their experience, and provide encouragement and support for their fellow Life Tree cultivators. Communications tools built into Mindbloom allow journaling about experiences, with an option to share those journal entries with varying degrees of privacy. Communication can range from sharing a journal entry with an entire Facebook community, or sending a solo snail mail to closest friends.

The objective of Mindbloom's Life Game is to grow the life you want by creating and maintaining a Life Tree where the branches represent the areas of life most important to you (e.g., health, spirituality, relationships, leisure, lifestyle, finances, creativity, and career), and the leaves represent specific goals, passions, or dreams.

By taking small steps toward those goals, passions, or dreams on a regular basis (e.g. drink eight glasses of water per day), you will not only grow and maintain a healthy tree (and life!), but you will earn seeds (i.e., points) you can spend on additional branches, leaves, and actions. And, as you earn more seeds, your tree will automatically be "upgraded" to new environments.

Like life itself, the Mindbloom's Life Game is not about the end result, but about the journey. Goals, passions, and dreams will continually change, but as long as you are taking small steps everyday and having fun, then you've already won!

How was Mindbloom created? The seeds of Mindbloom were planted in the spring of 2007. The company's cofounders Chris Hewett and Brent Poole incorporated Mindbloom in 2008, and a year later, it welcomed its first online community members.

Chris' decade-long experience with game development, coupled with Brent's business acumen, suggested how they might help others change and grow. "Why not extend this application into an online service?" they thought. "A visually compelling, motivational experience that could inspire individuals to reach for their dreams." Their own journeys taught them that significant change is always possible, but only when there's some fun in it, when it unfolds in small, manageable steps, and when there's plenty of encouragement from family, friends, and even personal coaches and trainers. Mindbloom, therefore, was designed to be the kind of entertaining education I mentioned earlier.

Mindbloom's lively atmosphere, visually playful interface, and small surprises within the Mindbloom experience motivate members to grow along eight branches of life: career, creativity, leisure, lifestyle, money, relationships, spirituality, and health.

What are the benefits of the Mindbloom experience? The key benefits people report are that Mindbloom reminds them daily of the kind of person they want to be—the kind of spouse, parent, employee, and community member who does the right thing most of the time, and aspires to do well every single day. Mindbloom serves as a conduit for encouragement and support that also makes it fun to live fully and consciously. And, it evolves with you. Your Life Tree can change as you change, to grow and flourish in new directions, while old growth can be pruned away when that growth segment is complete. Because every Life Tree is unique and crafted by hand by the person whose life it represents, Life Trees become highly valued—almost sacred to their creators. Most valuable of all, communities form around these growth experiences. We all know we work harder when someone is watching, and Mindbloom not only lets us watch but also allows us to shout out encouragement and support to others in a meaningful and personalized manner, whether shouting from the rooftops to your online communities or whispering to your closest confidantes within the confines of your most personal, private, and protected branches.

Mindbloom provides the perfect framework for making our heart's desires known while keeping us moving in the right direction with intention and integrity. To better position yourself to invest in your dreams, passions, and future, visit Mindbloom today at www.Mindbloom.com.

Mindbloom is just one unique way you can take ownership for your thoughts, your actions, and the resultant changes that you experience. Whether you use this application, or my free goal sheets, or some other format, what is important is conscious living. Daily mindfulness helps us to keep our best intentions and desired outcomes at the forefront of our lives, and the net result is a sense of purpose, productivity, and personal satisfaction.

EXERCISE

List five ways you can and will commit to better investing in yourself.

1. _____
   _____
   _____

2. _____
   _____
   _____

3. _____
   _____
   _____

4. _____
   _____
   _____
   _____

5. _____
   _____
   _____
   _____

AFFLUENT ENTREPRENEUR PROFILE
JOHN D. ROCKEFELLER

John D. Rockefeller was born in 1839 in Richford, New York. When he was 14, he moved with his family to Cleveland, Ohio. During his teen years, he strongly believed in the importance of investing in himself. As a result, he started buying and selling meat, grain, and produce and was quick to make a profit. In the 1850s, Mr. Rockefeller met Samuel Adams who was an industrial chemist. Together they discussed a new way to cleanse oil with sulfuric acid. This was the beginning of Rockefeller getting into the oil business.

By 1870, Rockefeller and his friend Henry Flagler established a joint-stock corporation and named it Standard Oil with $1 million in investment funds. Soon Standard Oil started buying out other oil companies including Union Oil. After the Civil War, Standard Oil was eventually able to own and control 90 percent of the refined oil in the United States.

Soon issues arose with the railroads regarding transportation of the oil. Therefore, Rockefeller believed that instead of relying solely on the railroads for oil transportation, his company would make intensive infrastructure investments to build their own pipelines. The first

(continued)

(*continued*)

pipelines were built in Buffalo and Cleveland, and eventually, Rockefeller built pipelines right alongside the railroads, ironically reminding them that they were losing his business by not transporting his oil.

Once the automobile became more popular and accessible to mass numbers of Americans, the demand for Rockefeller's fuel skyrocketed, and by extension, so did his wealth for years to come. By today's dollar value, Rockefeller's wealth is estimated to have been equivalent to somewhere between $300 and $500 billion, which not only makes him the richest man in America in his day, but the richest man in all of American history.

John D. Rockefeller always tithed at church and also gave away money to many other organizations with his primary focus being education and other public health causes. He went on to establish his foundation and started giving away much of his money, including $80 million to the University of Chicago, funding to establish Spellman College, a major endowment to Johns Hopkins and many, many others.

SUMMARY

Anyone who has ever achieved any significant feat in life is quick to point out that while the education he received in school laid the foundation, it was the real-life education he received from hands-on learning that taught him how to make money. By being willing to invest in himself starting in his teen years, John D. Rockefeller is a perfect example of how self-education leads to wealth.

Today more entertainment options than ever before are vying for your time. I challenge you to make sure you don't spend the rest of your days purely in entertainment mode, but that you do what you can to lessen the gap between entertainment hours and your education and self-investment hours.

One of the best ways to invest in yourself is to soul search for your passions, rediscover your ultimate dreams, and invest in tools and resources to support your goals. One of the best resources I have found to help you achieve your goals, while still being entertaining, is Mindbloom. The small monthly fee to use it is nothing compared to the return on investment you will realize as you find yourself on the right track to achieving your goal of becoming an Affluent Entrepreneur.

Marketing Your Business Instead of Advertising It

No matter how substandard you feel your skill or talent may be, if you never produce your art, the world will always remain deprived of it.
—Derek R. Audette

I n this chapter, you will learn how and where you should spend your limited budget, your time, and your money marketing your business. As you will read here, I have never been a big fan of advertising your business. I think it is both risky and expensive, and it often doesn't generate a single phone call or lead.

Marketing can be far less expensive (and sometimes even free), and it can create tremendous results for your business. I'm going to share with you how and where to allocate your marketing budget, and I will offer you ideas so you can better market your business. You will also learn numerous no-cost marketing techniques. Finally, I will profile and share real-life examples of how the founder of one of the most successful restaurant chains in the United States took on the biggest restaurant in the world and received millions of dollars in free publicity as a result. The Affluent Entrepreneur often has to out-think the competition in order for his or her business to get the necessary publicity to achieve its financial goals.

THE DIFFERENCE BETWEEN MARKETING AND ADVERTISING

Every guru today has his own definition for the most frequently used terms in business, and I guess to some extent, I am no different. Of course, we would all agree that marketing and advertising are components of the same business plan. Furthermore, advertising is a component of marketing. However, I like to keep the two actions completely separate. Why? Because I believe one works and the other does not.

Let me explain by first asking you a few questions. Do you have deep pockets to throw away your money on advertising? Do you have a limited budget to market your business? Have you ever taken out a print ad in a newspaper, a commercial on radio or television, and yet never received a single phone call? Not one single call? Well, if the answer is what I think it is, then welcome to the club. Struggling Entrepreneurs don't know any better so they throw their money away on advertising.

By contrast, Affluent Entrepreneurs know that advertising does not work, so they invest their time, energies, and resources into marketing. Why? Because advertising is very expensive and often does not work. On the other hand, marketing is less expensive (sometimes even free) and works more times than not. Below are five examples of each, with the negatives of advertising above and the positive alternatives of marketing below:

Advertising (minuses)

- Taking out an ad in a newspaper (costly)

- Paying for a 30-second or 60-second spot on the radio (costly)

- Purchasing an infomercial on TV (costly)

- Getting ad banners on web sites (costly)

- Purchasing sponsorships for events (costly)

- Sending out direct mail pieces (costly)

Marketing (pluses)

+ Being interviewed in an article in the newspaper (free publicity)

+ Being featured as a radio guest on a talk radio show (free publicity)

+ Being a guest on a talk show or news show on TV (free publicity)

+ Doing social networking on the Internet (free)

+ Showing up to an event early and staying late to network (free)

+ Posting flyers on bulletin boards in high-traffic areas (free)

Marketing is the best way you can get publicity for your business. According to Dictionary.com, publicity is defined as, "An extensive mention in the news media or by word-of-mouth or other means of communications." Getting publicity is one of the secrets Affluent Entrepreneurs use in their businesses to grow their revenues. These revenues are not so much the result of increased sales due to the publicity, but rather increased credentials and proof among your current prospects, showing them exactly the value of your offerings.

As you can see from the above comparison, advertising costs a bunch of money while marketing does not. Also as you can see, marketing leads to opportunities for more publicity while advertising does not. However, some marketing will cost you money, but in these cases, the money is well worth it. I have one business partner who gets upward of 5 million looks on Facebook for as little as $200 invested. I think that is a solid reach for what he gets in return compared to spending $200 on a local ad in a community paper that you can only hope at best 10,000 readers will see. I think you get the point.

My experience with Facebook advertising has been an amazing one as well. Your ability to target who will see your ad on the other end makes me consider this strategy to be more of a hybrid model of both marketing and advertising than just pure advertising. The numbers are too big to comprehend, so let me just share with you what I experienced after just three days with my Facebook ads: 500,000 impressions of my ad on others' Facebook pages, and 75 of these folks clicked through to my web site, and my cost was about $50. Never in my career have I ever done anything (perhaps with the exception of being featured as the cover story in *USA TODAY*) that led to 500,000 people seeing my book cover. I am so impressed with Facebook's ad campaign that I definitely think you should implement it as part of your marketing strategy if you have not already done so.

Two no-cost or low-cost ways I have used to market my business with great success are public speaking and writing a book. Think about how easy and overlooked these two strategies are.

When you are a public speaker, you may have hundreds if not thousands of captive buying minds in the audience, all intrigued with your message and ready to buy your service.

How about writing and publishing a book? With *Creating Your Own Destiny*, I sold more than 150,000 copies of my book in five languages all over the world. Well, each one of those books has become a "sales-it"—not a salesman or saleswoman since a book is gender-neutral. Each book becomes a marketing tool delivering my company's products or services to potential buyers all over the world. What other marketing tool do you know that can generate interest in your business at such a low cost?

Often, I run into struggling entrepreneurs who are spending $3,000 to $5,000 per month, year after year, advertising their businesses. I encourage these folks to become Affluent Entrepreneurs by writing, publishing, and marketing their books for a fraction of what they would spend on advertising. Perhaps best of all, the shelf life of a newspaper is 2 to 5 days, whereas the shelf life of a book can be 100 years or more. Consider writing a book to use as your best way to market your business.

EXERCISE

Now think for a moment of how you can better introduce your product or services to the masses, and list below five low-cost or no-cost marketing strategies you can implement right away to drive additional revenues to your bottom line.

1. _____
   _____
   _____

2. _____
   _____
   _____

3. _____
   _____
   _____

4. _____
   _____
   _____

5. _____
   _____
   _____

AFFLUENT ENTREPRENEUR PROFILE
S. TRUETT CATHY

Now let me give you an example of someone who understood the difference between marketing and advertising, and used that knowledge to take his business to the top and become a billionaire in the process. S. Truett Cathy is known as God's billionaire due to his belief that

(continued)

(*continued*)

his employees needed to be home on Sundays with their families. As a result, his Chick-fil-A restaurants are all closed on Sundays.

Mr. Cathy's challenge all along has been competing with other restaurants that seemingly have unlimited budgets to advertise their businesses. For example, one insider reports that McDonald's Restaurants spend more than $2 billion per year on advertising. As a result, S. Truett knew all along that trying to advertise to compete with McDonald's was a big waste of money; he didn't want to throw his money away in his quest to create the world's best chicken sandwich. So he focused exclusively on chicken sandwiches while others tried to serve a little of this and a little of that, only to dilute their brands.

Instead, Chick-fil-A spent a small amount of money on clever billboards around Atlanta displaying images of cows painting on a billboard the message, "Eat Mor Chikin" and "Five out of Five Cows Agree, Eat Mor Chikin." As a result, his company received millions of dollars worth of free publicity via radio, newspapers, and TV because Chick-fil-A had successfully created a publicity buzz. Advertising dollars couldn't have bought the level of good publicity Chick-fil-A received from the media.

Today, it is a common opinion that the best chicken sandwiches on the planet are made by Atlanta-based Chick-fil-A. If you have not had one, do yourself a favor on your travels and treat yourself to one of these sandwiches. These successful results were realized all because the visionary behind the company understood that to succeed in business you must focus your efforts on marketing, not on advertising. I challenge you to implement this marketing strategy in your business so you can also become an Affluent Entrepreneur.

Mr. Cathy went on to build an empire of over 1,300 restaurants and has amassed a net worth of close to $1.5 billion. However, for him it has never been about the money. It has been about the people in his life whom he could help out: his family, his employees, and the 150 foster children to whom he has served as "Grandpa." His efforts were all generated by his desire to make this world a better place.

I have the honor of calling Mr. Samuel Truett Cathy my friend. Around 2002 or so, I attended the National Speakers Association workshop in Portland, Oregon, where I exhibited my self-published version of *Creating Your Own Destiny*. I met some pretty amazing speakers and entrepreneurs at this event.

At the time, since we don't have Chick-fil-As in Washington state, I didn't know who this man was. So there I was manning my booth when all of a sudden this older man came up to me and commented on how impressed he was that I had sold 40,000 copies of my book in the first six months of its release. He was so nice and polite; we chatted for 5 to 10 minutes and later rode in the elevator together.

Before he departed my booth, he advised me that he hadn't brought his wallet with him so he was unable to purchase a copy of my book. He advised me that he too was an author, and if I would trust him, he said that when he got home he would send me a copy of his book in trade. Still not knowing who he really was, I agreed to do so, assuming I would never hear from him again.

To my surprise, about a week later I received a package from S. Truett Cathy with a signed copy of his book inside. He signed his book: "To Patrick, My friend I loved your book and I enjoyed meeting you." Then he

(continued)

(*continued*)

signed his name "God Bless You, S. Truett Cathy" and also inscribed a powerful Proverbs quote from the Bible. To this day, his book remains one of my most prized possessions, and I have given his marketing/advertising Chick-fil-A story as an example in over 500 of my speeches. And to this day, whenever I speak in the south-eastern part of the United States, I always make it a point to go out of my way to enjoy the best chicken sandwiches on the planet.

SUMMARY

The bottom line is this. If you have an unlimited budget to grow your business, then congratulations on your inherited wealth or your excess cash flow. If you find yourself in this position, feel free to spend all the money you want on advertising your business.

However, if you are like me and most other entrepreneurs who have a limited budget to market their businesses, then I strongly encourage you to focus your time, energy, and money on marketing your business instead of advertising.

My only exception to this rule would be to test-market some online advertising such as Facebook and perhaps some others. As a result of focusing on marketing instead of advertising, not only will your business thrive, but your cash flow will dramatically improve as well. One of my all-time favorite concepts in regard to wealth creation is that it doesn't matter how much money you make; what matters is how much money you keep.

Therefore, I challenge you both in your personal life and in your business life to make a decision to keep "some" of all the money you make. I believe this marketing philosophy will help you to do just that.

I am hopeful that you have been inspired by Mr. Cathy's model, his vision, and his courage to stay closed on Sundays due to his faith. He is an inspiration to me and will be for the rest of my life. I hope his profile above will inspire you not only to become an Affluent Entrepreneur, but also to be so much more so you can give back to the world and become a blessing to mankind.

Creating Walk-Away Incomes

I am always doing what I cannot do yet,
in order to learn how to do it.
—Vincent van Gogh

In this chapter, you will learn why it's essential to invest in yourself, your systems, and your business model to earn and create residual, walk-away incomes. You'll see that by using this principle in your life and in your business, you'll truly become the Affluent Entrepreneur and achieve prosperity in the free enterprise system. You will also learn how to price your products and services, and more importantly, how to collect from those clients. You will be introduced to a monthly royalty pay plan model that you may decide to replicate, plus you will learn how and why Mary Kay Ash from Mary Kay Cosmetics is honored as a leading female entrepreneur in American history.

The number one question I hear from my clients is this: "How should I charge for my services?" My answer is simple: charge and accept whatever the client is willing to pay! What do I mean by this? People may purchase the same product or service from different stores or online retailers and each pay a slightly different price. That is just the way things work. For example, you could call Marriott directly to book a hotel room and may pay $250 per night in a big city; yet if you booked it through Priceline. com, the same hotel room may cost you $139 per night.

Therefore, I firmly believe you, as a small business owner and Affluent Entrepreneur, need to somewhere, somehow post your fees. As a professional speaker and publishing and book marketing coach I post my fees on my web site for visitors to see. Does this mean everyone will pay the same amount? As much as I would like to say that is the case, it is certainly not.

One of my mentors once taught me to accept whatever the customer is willing to pay, on whatever terms the customer is willing to agree. Now as the business owner, and Affluent Entrepreneur, you can always say "No" and counter the customer's discounted offer. I turn away potential clients almost daily. It drives me crazy when people continuously try to gain intellectual property without paying a few extra dollars for it.

As a coach or consultant, I always offer virtually anyone a "complimentary" 30–60 minute consultation. Why 30–60 minutes? If I like the person I will give 60, if I don't, I will try and cut him off somewhere around 30 minutes and move on. Next! Someone else is waiting. This is the mantra you need to develop.

The key is that during this complimentary consultation, you tell the person "what" he needs to do, but you don't give him the resources on "how" to do it until the person becomes your client and actually pays for the service. For example as a publishing coach, I will tell a prospective author that he needs to write the manuscript, get it edited, proofread, typeset, acquire an ISBN number, hire a cover designer, buy a bar code, get the book printed, find a distributor, list the book on Amazon, and so on—almost overwhelming him with too much information. Then the person will realize the importance and value of my service. Once the customer hires me, I will then always give him or her all the resources needed to get the job done. These resources include personal introductions, names, phone numbers, e-mail addresses, and the next step in the process. You need to do the same. Tell your customers the "what" and then offer them the "how" after they hire you for the job.

So, now you know that you need to post your fees, knowing your prospects are going to negotiate with you. If you are rolling in money, and have more clients than you know what to do with, then you don't need to negotiate; you can just say, "No thank you" and move on. If they are serious, they will come back and pay you the higher amount almost every time.

Conversely, if you are starving and don't have all the clients you desire, then often you need to accept the person's offer and bring him on as client based on whatever he can afford or whatever is in his budget.

Next is the form of payment. How and what forms of payment do I offer, and what should you offer? Bottom line, if you are serious about becoming an Affluent Entrepreneur, you need to accept all of the following forms of payment (in this order):

1. Money order or cashier's check (guaranteed funds)

2. Personal check (no fees for processing)

3. Visa, MasterCard, Discover, Amex*

Most of my clients pay either by check or credit card. I advise them that I prefer a check, but I will also accept credit cards. You should do the same.

Finally, is it better to accept payments or to get the money all upfront? My rule of thumb is *always* to do what you can to be paid in full, 100 percent upfront. Often, whether for speaking or for publishing coaching, I will even give a generous 10–25 percent discount for paying in advance. When clients pay 100 percent upfront, you know they are serious and mean business.

While this model is good, the downside of this payment or collections model is that once your client is paid in full, you no longer have other revenue coming in from this client unless she continues to buy more products or services from you. Therefore, always collect 100 percent upfront (whenever you can), but build a back-end residual/royalty program.

---

* Convenient, but the merchant-processing fees are expensive.

What is a back-end residual/royalty model? It means you perform the services ongoing and then get paid for the rest of your life. I suspect many of you reading this book are in the info-preneuring business, meaning that you market your intellectual property for a fee. It could be books, speaking, coaching, consulting, or any other number of services that fall into this category. The goal is to build something once and then get paid for it the rest of your life.

The direct sales industry has mastered this model. Many, many millionaires come out of the network marketing industry because they see the power of this model and put it to use in their lives. Now, I am not saying that you have to join a network marketing company; what I am saying is to apply this knowledge to your business model. Also, study the business models of some of today's most successful direct selling companies, and then apply this royalty income model to your business so you can quickly build your company's revenue streams. Having multiple streams of income under your platform of wealth creation is a viable way to meet more people, learn from others, and leverage the opportunities and trends in the marketplace so you can further grow your complete business model.

Another option is to create your own program where you market a product or service and have customers pay you a small monthly fee for the rest of their lives. For example, let me tell you about my Inner Circle club.

INNER CIRCLE

Several years ago when I founded www.BestSellerBookCoaching .com, I started offering my clients a weekly 8 AM PST publishing coaching Inner Circle mastermind call. In the early days of this call, we may have had only 2 or 3 people per week on the call, but now we have grown to having regularly 30 to 40 people on each call. My Inner Circle callers ask questions, and I provide real-life answers and concrete examples that they can apply to their businesses. Think about it: If I had to coach these 40 people one on one and repeat myself with each of these clients, it would take me 40 hours on the phone to achieve this goal.

However, by leveraging technology via the conference call line, I can coach a whole lot more people all at once, and you can do the same. Long story short, this call quickly became a client favorite where people could get up early on Monday and start diving into their book projects.

As a result of the success of this call, I have launched my Inner Circle call, which takes place every Monday at 12:30 PM PST. Of course, these calls are recorded, so if my clients can't listen in at the designated time, they can have a link e-mailed to them so they can listen whenever it's convenient for them.

The goal of the call is to offer clients four one-hour inspirational calls per month live over the phone. That is four hours per month total with each client paying $12.95 per month on a credit card for the rest of his or her life. So let's do the math; soon I will be at 1,000 subscribers and it will equate to $12,950 per month of residual royalty monthly income. Imagine what it feels like each month to know that no matter what else happens, you automatically have $13,000 coming into your bank account.

Okay, so let's stretch our minds a bit. My next goal is to achieve 10,000 members subscribing to my Inner Circle program at $12.95 per month. Isn't that a residual royalty income of $129,500 per month? I believe so, and consequently, I've made it my goal for my Inner Circle club. You can do the same. In the beginning it will be slow, but over time, it will all be worth it.

EXERCISE

What are three new ideas you can implement in your business to create royalty/residual income into your bank account?

1. _____

_____

_____

2. _____

    _____

    _____

3. _____

    _____

    _____

COLLECTIONS

By no means am I a seasoned collections officer, nor have I ever worked in the collections industry before. But I can say this— regardless of your hesitation to call people when they owe you money, it is something you MUST get into the habit of doing. Call your clients who owe you money; make them an offer to accept less, and you will be amazed at how willing they will be to pay you what they can when you do.

Also note that some people are just going to have things happen in their lives that may inhibit their ability to pay. These events may include divorce, job loss, or a half-dozen other things. Think about it; if you went through some of these difficulties, you would want people to take it easy on you.

Therefore, look at the person's situation, walk a mile in his or her shoes, and then make a decision as to whether or not to collect. If the person has the means, then go right ahead and do the best you can to collect on the debts owed; if not, forgive the debt and move on. Pursuing it may not be worth your time and effort.

AFFLUENT ENTREPRENEUR PROFILE
MARY KAY ASH

Mary Kay Ash was born Mary Kathlyn Wagner in Houston, Texas, in 1918. She did all of her formal school-ing in Houston, including attending the University of

Houston. She was soon married, had three children, and then divorced. Needing to support herself, she began her sales career for Stanley Home Products, a direct selling company based out of Houston. After 25 years of being in sales, she left this company out of frustration because an individual she had trained was unfairly promoted over her.

Mary then retired and set out to write a book that would explain her ideal way to run a business. The book was so successful that it became the blueprint for her business plan, and as a result, she and her second husband successfully launched Mary Kay Cosmetics in 1963 with an investment of $5,000. Soon thereafter, she opened her first storefront in Dallas, Texas.

Eventually, Mary Kay saw the power that the direct selling business model would have both in attracting additional marketers for her product and in its ability to increase her sales. As a result the company continued to grow, and after a 1979 interview with *60 Minutes* on CBS her organization's sales soared to record numbers.

Mary Kay's vision was to create a pay plan, business model in which representatives could only get promoted as a result of helping others to achieve their goals. Hence, she became an advocate of the Golden Rule to "treat others as you wish to be treated." She preached her core values of God first, family second, and career third, and encouraged all in her organization to keep their lives in balance. Her top sales achievers in the company were rewarded with pink Cadillacs that made them easily recognized as successful.

By creating this walk-away and royalty income model, Mary Kay built a system to help others achieve their goals by helping her achieve her own. In 2008, Mary Kay Cosmetics had grown to a company doing roughly $2.5 billion per year in sales from 1.7 million associates in nearly 40 countries throughout the world.

SUMMARY

The purpose of this chapter is to challenge you to study and evaluate how you as an entrepreneur earn your money. Do you collect your money like most business owners do where you get paid one time for performing a product or a service, meaning that every time you perform that service, your client is now done paying you?

Or do you think there is some value to earning money using a royalty/residual model that authors use with their books, those in financial services use such as with insurance, or the direct selling industry uses where you do the work once, but you get paid for a lifetime? If you fully understand how this model works, you will be able to tweak your company's product or service slightly and then train your customers to pay you a small amount, month after month, for the rest of their lives. This model is one the insurance industry uses, and I know a lot of Affluent Entrepreneurs in that business.

If you are struggling for a way to create residual income in your business model, brainstorm with yourself or others in your business about how you can insert a royalty income stream into your model. Perhaps consider offering an Inner Circle program as I have suggested in this chapter that would bring revenue to your business month after month, without your having to start out at zero sales again each month.

Next, as an Affluent Entrepreneur, you must be flexible by accepting whatever your clients are willing to pay you for your product or service. If you stay firm to a rigid pricing model, you will lose revenue. If you remain flexible and allow your prospects more involvement in determining the amounts they can afford, you will earn a lot more sales, thus resulting in more revenue to your bottom line.

Finally, if you truly want to create walk-away income, then be bold and get very good at writing invoices, sending invoices, and collecting on these invoices. Once you master this role, you will be in good shape. Sending the invoice, agreement, or proposal to the prospect is the final step in closing the sale. As you master this skill, you will be one step closer to becoming an Affluent Entrepreneur.

Selling Your Business and Starting Over Again

I am doing this because I want to do it better.
—Walt Disney

Now that you have come to the end of this book, you may wonder what is your next step as an Affluent Entrepreneur. Hopefully, by now you realize that you do indeed have what it takes to put these strategies, ideas, and suggestions to use in your business. I sincerely believe if you apply these 20 proven principles to your business, *you* will become an Affluent Entrepreneur. In this chapter, you are going to learn about what is next in your life and whether or not you should sell your business and start over again. You will also learn how Kirk Kerkorian made $660 million in one day.

WHAT'S NEXT?

Perhaps you have come as far as you can on this journey by yourself, so now it is time to partner with additional resources, bigger players, and organizations that have resources, distribution, contacts, and systems in place that would take you years and years to try and build on your own.

In other words, if you feel you are at a point where your business has become stagnant and you need fresh ideas, more capital, or just a change of scenery, perhaps now is the time to sell your business and start over again by pursuing the next passion on your list.

When I travel the world speaking, I always challenge my readers to take an inventory of their passions and write down the five activities they most love to do. I encourage you to do the same. When I recently went through this same process, it led to my decision to seek the resources of a world-class publisher when I sold the rights to my book to John Wiley & Sons, Inc.

Prior to this deal happening, I had spent every waking moment promoting my book and speaking business, ultimately giving 1,500 speaking engagements through North America and Europe and selling an estimated 150,000 copies of my book in five languages (in fact, I suspect foreign publishers continually sandbag their numbers so it is virtually impossible to know the actual number). Heck, based on the number of e-mails I get from Nigeria alone, I wouldn't be surprised if I've sold a quarter of a million copies just in that country.

My point is that I felt after 10 years of promoting my book, I had done just about everything I could do on my own and now I needed help from the big boys. I have been on the cover of *USA TODAY*, been featured in the *New York Times*, have been on TV, and have given over 400 radio interviews in Europe, North America, Australia, and New Zealand. All this, yet I still hadn't achieved my goal of selling one million copies of my book.

Additionally, I launched www.BestSellerBookCoaching.com in 2002 and have since helped nearly 250 people to publish their books. Even with all of my accolades, however, some authors would tell me they were not interested in my publishing coaching services because they wanted to hold out for a traditional publishing deal. I told them to hold on tight because they might be holding on for the rest of their lives. So when the opportunity presented itself, I decided to sign the paperwork with John Wiley & Sons, Inc., to have them take over the rights of both my first book,

Creating Your Own Destiny, and my second book, *The Affluent Entrepreneur*.

As discussed earlier in the book, John Wiley & Sons, Inc., is a $3 billion, 200-year old company, so I figured it would be able to take my books to a bigger platform, quicker, with better quality and a proven name behind the brand. After doing all the research to find the right traditional publisher, I discovered the three following key points that helped me make my decision to sell the rights to my books.

First, by teaming up with this world-class organization and its 200-year old distribution system, I could achieve my goal of 1 million copies sold much quicker than by going solo.

Two, I realized that by partnering with Wiley, I could strengthen my brand name and attract even more speaking engagements due to the book purchases that would be made and the familiarity created by my book sitting on the shelves in bookstores worldwide.

Three, I realized that the partnership with Wiley would also bring my publishing coaching business even more credibility, because now I would have the credentials to counsel my clients not only on how to self-publish but also on how to position themselves to attract the attention of a traditional book publisher if that was a direction they wished to pursue.

Combined, all three of these reasons made the decision to publish with John Wiley & Sons, Inc., a no-brainer, so in the summer of 2009, I signed a two-book deal with them. This business decision was one of the best I have ever made, and all three of the above scenarios have come true as a result of this new partnership.

I encourage you to complete the exercises below to see whether you feel that now is the right time to sell your business and to start over again pursuing your new passions.

EXERCISE A

What resources are you missing with your business that would allow you to create a global impact if they were at your disposal?

1. _____

_____

_____

2. _____

_____

_____

3. _____

_____

_____

EXERCISE B

In the spaces below, write down the top three buyers you suspect would be interested in purchasing your business.

1. _____

2. _____

3. _____

EXERCISE C

Now write out three benefits you would experience in your life as a result of selling your business or having another ownership group take your business to the next level.

1. _____

2. _____

3. _____

TO CASH IN OR HOLD OUT

Selling your business may very well be one of the most difficult decisions you will ever need to make in your life. The reason is you have been building your business successfully all these years, so while part of you thinks that now is the time to sell, another bit of self-talk is telling you to hold on to it for years to come.

I remember in my early working years how I would have interviews with different companies and then try to figure out whether I should stay with my employer or move on to the next opportunity. It was always one of the most difficult decisions. At one point, I was an Account Manager for Avis Rent A Car, selling corporate car contracts to major corporations in competition with Hertz and Budget. I made a killing on the sales; after all, who hasn't heard of Avis ("We Try Harder"). All I had to do was show up, have a contract in hand, and offer my buyer a guaranteed one dollar less cost than Hertz in all class sizes of cars, and I would sign the customer.

My territory was all of Washington State and Alaska. However, the best part of my job was I would get a brand-new company car, literally as often as I wanted one. I had contacts down at the airport who had me on speed dial, and when the new load of cars came in on the big trucks, I would have them select my favorite color car, put it aside, and then I would come down the next day and trade in my six-week-old car for a brand-new one. The money wasn't the best, but the perks were incredible. Furthermore, I had a really cool Regional Sales Manager, and I also liked our VP of Sales. I was hooked and in love with Avis. To this day, I still rent exclusively from Avis when I am on the road speaking.

So what was my problem? I got a job offer in high-tech sales that paid me double my current salary. I spent a couple of weeks trying to decide whether to change jobs, and finally, I created a graph to show all the positive and negative things about each position at both companies. The reason I am sharing this story with you is that I think you need to do the same when deciding whether or not to sell. Therefore, in the exercise below, complete the thoughts and weigh the benefits of each to assist you in your business decision.

EXERCISE D

1. Which opportunity can best meet your long-term financial needs?

   _____

2. Which opportunity will allow you to spend more time with your family?

   _____

3. Which opportunity will allow you to expand your footprint and grow globally?

   _____

4. Which opportunity will give you more personal freedom in life?

   _____

5. Which opportunity does your spouse think is best for the family?

   _____

Whether it be a new job or keeping/selling your business, asking yourself these kinds of questions and filling out a +/- graph to compare your options will best help you make this decision. Finally, ask yourself which way your heart is telling you to lean. With this gut instinct, make a decision and stick to it, move on, and enjoy the next step on your journey.

Looking at your choice, you need to be able to determine, if you are going to sell, whether now is the right time. Are the new owners capable of helping you create a global footprint for your product or service? Sooner or later, we all realize we can do only so much. Then it's time to bring in experts who can help us move our business to the level where our product or service becomes a household name. Understanding this principle is essential because proper execution of it will set you up for life and ensure your financial future, even allowing you to decide whether you will ever work in your own business again. If you understand this principle, then there's no question or doubt—you *will* become an Affluent Entrepreneur!

AFFLUENT ENTREPRENEUR PROFILE
KIRK KERKORIAN

Kirk Kerkorian was born in 1917 in Fresno, California, to Armenian immigrant parents. As a child, he dreamt of one day being a pilot, and he did achieve this goal, learning to fly and working with the British Air Force Ferry Command during World War II. Kerkorian saved all his earnings during the war, and when it was over, he bought his own airplane. Soon thereafter, he purchased his own airline and was soon shuttling gamblers from Los Angeles to Las Vegas.

Once familiar with the Vegas scene, Kerkorian started investing in land in Las Vegas. In 1962, he bought 80 acres of land across the strip from the Flamingo for $960,000 and later sold it to Caesar's for $9 million. This deal went so well that he did it again, this time buying 82 acres in Vegas and reselling them for yet another huge profit. In 1969, he bought the MGM Grand properties in both Vegas and Reno and then sold them to Bally's in 1986 for $594 million.

With much of the money he made in real estate, Kerkorian started purchasing huge amounts of stock in different automobile manufacturers, including major stakes in GM, Chrysler, and Ford. When Chrysler announced it would merge with the German automobile manufacturer Daimler-Benz, Kerkorian made $660 million. This sum

(continued)

(*continued*)

represented the increased value in his stock from May 5 to May 6, 1998. At the time, he was 81 years old and still making deals happen.

Through his shrewd Las Vegas real estate transactions, and by playing his cards right with U.S. auto manufacturers, Kerkorian amassed a net worth of $16 billion, according to *Forbes*. What is most impressive about his story is that his foundation has given away hundreds of millions of dollars, and yet he refuses to allow anything to be named in his honor.

SUMMARY

One of my friends in the real estate business once taught me that everything in the marketplace is for sale even if there is not a sign in front of it. For the right price, often the owner will sell. Therefore, keep your house in order and your business ready to sell at any time; you never know when the opportunity will present itself.

Once you have a deal on the table, carefully consider all the advantages and disadvantages. Include your family in the discussion and in the decision. At the end of the day, make a decision, act quickly, and have no regrets. Do whatever you think will allow you to scale your business on a global level to impact as many people as possible. Do what you think will make you an Affluent Entrepreneur and empower you to give of your time and money.

After the transaction has been completed, go on vacation, take time off, pursue your passions, and volunteer your time and money to help those in need. Then, once you get bored, write up a new business plan and start over again, building your new business a better way.

Passing It On and Giving It Away

The only time you mustn't fail is the last time you try.
—Charles Kettering

Hopefully, as a result of reading this book, you have now come to the same conclusion I have come to—achieving wealth for your family and becoming an Affluent Entrepreneur is not solely for others but also for you. I wrote this book to prove to you that with the right skill set (which you can learn and apply to your business) YOU can and will become the Affluent Entrepreneur I have described in this book.

I have always liked the following three questions that I ask my clients: (1) If not you, then who? Someone is going to achieve your dreams, why not you! (2) If not this, then what? If not business ownership, what other financial vehicle are you aware of that can set you free to achieve the life you have always wanted? (3) If not now, then when? When is there a better time than right now, today, to take action on your visions and move forward pursuing the results that only an Affluent Entrepreneur can achieve?

The point of these questions is clear—being an Affluent Entrepreneur is the way you can achieve your dreams, have security for your family and yourself, and live the life you desire and deserve. You are the one who can and will become an Affluent Entrepreneur. Business ownership is the right financial vehicle, and *now* is the time to make it happen!

When you apply the thoughts, suggestions, and lessons offered in this book, you truly become an unstoppable force that is fully capable of achieving all you desire in life. You become the Affluent Entrepreneur. You are the driving force that overcomes all obstacles and all adversities. You become the dominant force in your life that predetermines your future. You become the Affluent Entrepreneur you have always secretly dreamed and known you could be.

Will it be easy? No. Are there going to be adversities that will come into your life? Of course. Do you have what it takes to apply the lessons of business and life to your particular situation? Absolutely. Every talent you have, every resource you need, every vision you can create, every ounce of belief required—they are all waiting within you, waiting only for your subconscious mind to make that life-changing decision to get everything it is that you really want out of life.

Once you achieve this milestone of becoming an Affluent Entrepreneur, you will achieve true freedom. You will create a world-class product or service that can change the world. You will be able to be there for your family. You will be able to travel the world. You will be able to help those in your life who need your financial assistance. You will be able to empower others to take control of their lives. You will be the parent your kids want and need. When you apply this book to your life and your business, you will get exactly what you want both in your life and in your work.

However, none of this will just happen unless you take action. One of my mentors, Harvey Mackay, has always said, "Ideas without actions are worthless!"

In other words, you can become the Affluent Entrepreneur when you transform all of the principles in this book from theory and advice into action. See, I firmly believe the Law of Attraction actually works. Whatever you want, wants you back. You are a living magnet, and that which you want and believe you can obtain—you can attract it into your life, making your dream reality. When you create your desired thought, or desired outcome in your mind, your body and your hands physically mold whatever it is that you want out of life.

As Wayne Dyer has said, "You'll see it when you believe it."

So believe in what you want to have enter into your life. Imagine yourself being that successful Affluent Entrepreneur. First, keep doing what you're doing. If you didn't want to be an Affluent Entrepreneur, you wouldn't have reached the end of this book. You know you want it. You believe it can happen. Now go forward, holding on to your vision and taking the action to make it happen. The universe will meet you halfway, attracting to you the resources, people, events, and situations you need to make your dream a reality.

I challenge you to create that vision now. Take a look forward in your life and apply this book's hard-learned lessons to it. Think three to five years into the future, and ask yourself, *What do I want my future to be?* Once you have a crystal-clear focus of your future life, I challenge you to live your life today as if you have already achieved your desired outcome.

Don't wait—there is no such thing as tomorrow. Whether we realize it or not, we all have an expiration date. Just like spoiled milk, one day the time will come when we move on from this world, as we know it. Therefore, don't wait. I challenge you to take immediate action, overcome your self-limiting beliefs, and pursue the life you have always dreamed of living.

Don't feel limited by what path to take. Look at the Affluent Entrepreneurs I have profiled in this book—they came from all walks of life, white and black, male and female, and they made their money in different industries.

Here is a snapshot of the Affluent Entrepreneurs and their respective industries:

Affluent Entrepreneur	*Industry*
Mary Kay Ash	Direct Selling/Cosmetics
Richard Branson	Music/Airlines
Warren Buffett	Finance/Investing
Andrew Carnegie	Manufacturing/Steel
S. Truett Cathy	Restaurants
Henry Ford	Automobiles
Bill Gates	Computer Software
J. Paul Getty	Oil
H.L. Hunt	Oil
Kirk Kerkorian	Real Estate/Stock Market
Ralph Lauren	Clothing
Larry Page and Larry Brin	Internet
Ross Perot	Computer Software
John D. Rockefeller	Oil
Martha Stewart	Entertainment/Publishing
Donald Trump	Real Estate/Entertainment/Publishing/Education
Cornelius Vanderbilt	Shipping/Railroads/Transportation
Sam Walton	Retailing
Frederick Weyerhaeuser	Forestry/Real Estate
Oprah Winfrey	Entertainment/Publishing

Look at the diversity of these industries. If you are in one of these industries, perhaps you can learn from the Affluent Entrepreneur profiled for that industry. If not, perhaps you may need to select another industry. If so, perhaps you just need to keep on persisting until you succeed. Remember, there are a million ways to make a million (or even a billion) dollars . . . it just takes the "execution" of one way. . . .

I want to help you find that way, to be your coach, your confidant, your virtual mastermind member, and your accountability partner. If I can do it, so can you. I believe in you perhaps more than you believe in yourself.

Remember, though, as you become the Affluent Entrepreneur God intended you to be, there will be people out there envious of your success, people who will try to stop you in your tracks and to distract you from your vision. I feel sorry for these toxic people who will do anything possible to give you their awful plague. Avoid them. Eliminate them from your life. Understand that they are jealous of your success and want to pull you down to their levels. Don't go there. Never let their opinions impact your belief in what is possible and what is right for you. Understand that some people will like you, but some people won't. So what! What's next? Focus instead on what you want and need to do to have the success and happiness you desire. What is important is what you feel about yourself, not what others think of you!

Therefore, apply these 20 proven principles to your life and your business and you will achieve the prosperity you have always desired.

1. Create Your Own Unique Product or Service

2. Identify Hot Trends in the Marketplace

3. Get Your Family's Support

4. Apply the Principles of Successful Selling

5. Find and Hire the Right People

6. Develop a "No Matter What" Mentality

7. Participate in Mastermind Groups

8. Outsource Your Non–Revenue-Producing Tasks

9. Secure Win-Win Transactions

10. Leverage Technology and the Internet

11. Take Calculated Risks

12. Turn Adversity into Your University

13. Use Other People's Money

14. Prospect 50 Percent of Your Working Hours

15. Build Your Brand Identity

16. Hunt for Big Deals

17. Invest in Yourself

18. Market Your Business Instead of Advertising It

19. Create Walk-Away Incomes

20. Sell Your Business and Doing it Again

Once these principles are applied to your life, you will experience a level of momentum that will outperform any recession, any obstacle, and any roadblock. As an Affluent Entrepreneur, I believe that when you apply these principles to your business, you will be bulletproof. Not only will you be able to meet a recession head-on, but you will also mentally and financially choose not to participate in it. You will have all the resources you need at your disposal to become and stay an Affluent Entrepreneur. You will find yourself standing on the mountaintop, with your business as your foundation and only the sky as your limit.

We've all heard it's lonely at the top, but it doesn't have to be. Yes, it's true that money can't buy love. But you know by now that being an Affluent Entrepreneur isn't about just acquiring money. It's about being affluent in all areas of your life—rich in happiness, family, friends, and a desire to make the world a better place. Remember Ebenezer Scrooge? His riches only made him a miserable, lonely, old man. For him, it was lonely at the top. Sure he had wealth, but Scrooge didn't really become an Affluent Entrepreneur until he also became a philanthropist, until he dedicated his life to helping others, in sharing his wealth and more important, his love.

Affluent Entrepreneurs share their wealth, not just their money, but also their wealth of joy, experiences, and knowledge. Remember Andrew Carnegie? He gave away millions and millions of dollars before he died. It was his goal to give away all his money, but the universe kept that money pouring in for him so that he never ran out. That is the Law of Attraction working to provide abundance so it can be spread out. Among the wonderful gifts Carnegie left behind him are thousands of libraries in towns all over the globe. And look at John D. Rockefeller—he became the richest man in American history, and what did he do with his money? He endowed universities. In recent years, Bill and Melinda Gates have equally proven themselves to be philanthropists. They realized they had made more money than they, their children, grandchildren, and great-grandchildren could ever spend in their lifetimes, so the Gates family decided to use their wealth to make a difference in the world. Today, the Bill and Melinda Gates Foundation not only gives away money, but it shares Bill Gates' wealth of knowledge and experience. Aided by Warren Buffett who has joined them on the foundation's board of directors, Bill and Melinda Gates have truly made a difference in the world. Remember the old saying, "Give a man a fish and you feed him for a day. Teach a man to fish and you feed him for a lifetime." The Bill and Melinda Gates Foundation gives away computers—it provides people all over the world with communication—access to the greater world—to the possibilities that exist—and to technology that educates people so they can become self-sustaining, healthy, and happy human beings. Bill Gates has truly proven himself to be an Affluent Entrepreneur, both by creating a product that made him wealthy, but also by creating a product that has changed the way people do business for the better, and then using his experience and wealth to benefit the lives of people worldwide.

Although I personally have not yet been able to give away the amount of money I would like, giving is not solely about money. We can also give of our time and services. Over the last 10 to 20 years, I have volunteered thousands of hours of my time by speaking to our nation's youth at school and colleges, hoping to inspire them to take charge of their destinies and to become the leaders I know they are capable of becoming, just as I did when I had the fulfilling experience of speaking to the students at the

University of Rhode Island, as I mentioned earlier in this book. Receiving their letters of thanks and knowing I had a made a difference to their futures were far more reward than any money I could have been paid, and I believe that inspiring them and giving them the confidence to pursue their dreams will help them more than any amount of money I could have given to them. Therefore, I challenge you to reflect upon what it is you have to give to others, to your community, and to the world. If you find yourself in a position due to a challenging economy where you are unable to give your money, take an inventory of your skill set, and then volunteer and offer your time to help others in need.

I am reminded here of a story about Mother Teresa, which I think says it all. After she once gave a talk about her work in India, a wealthy man came up to her and offered to give her money for her cause. She replied, "I don't need your money. Instead, tomorrow go find someone who thinks he is alone and make him realize he is not." That's what being an Affluent Entrepreneur boils down to in the end: using our time and talents not only to make our lives richer, but to make life better for everyone. We can give our money, but also, our time, our compassion, and our talents to make the world better for everyone.

Remember in the beginning of this book I dismissed the myth that being affluent is evil by quoting Christ as saying he came to give life so we may have it abundantly? Well, God wants us to be prosperous, but he also expects us to be good stewards of the wealth that comes to us. Like the parable in the Bible of the talents, the more we are given, the more we are expected to give back. We can give in many ways, with our time, talent, and our money, and the more we give, the more we receive in ways we can scarcely imagine.

For if you give, you will get! Your gift will return to you in full and overflowing measure, pressed down, shaken together to make room for more, and running over. Whatever measure you use to give—large or small—will be used to measure what is given back to you. (Luke 6:38)

In this book's subtitle, I promised you that by following the principles presented here, you could achieve prosperity. I define "prosperity" as creating enough wealth in your life to achieve the freedom you need and desire to spend the rest of your life giving of both your time and money to those in need. Ultimately, I believe that is the true definition of prosperity. My hopes are that in having read this book, you will now not only become an Affluent Entrepreneur, but you will also achieve true prosperity in the process, allowing you to spend the rest of your life giving to others.

Will becoming an Affluent Entrepreneur be easy? No! Will there be obstacles in your way? Of course. Will people try their darncdest to deter you from achieving your goals? Absolutely. However, if you take just two things away from this book, remember these two thoughts, both of which I learned from my father: Fight like hell to keep your family together, and never give up under any circumstances, ever!

I hope you have been inspired by my thoughts, strategies, techniques, and ideas on becoming an Affluent Entrepreneur. I challenge you to take action on these strategies as well as taking action on the items you listed in the exercises. I especially hope you have enjoyed and been inspired by the 20 Affluent Entrepreneurs I have profiled in this book. I hope you will conclude as I have, that becoming an Affluent Entrepreneur is NOT about the money; it is about the ability to create freedom in your life so that you as an Affluent Entrepreneur can model the behaviors of these 20 Affluent Entrepreneurs, and virtually, give it all away to those in need, just as these entrepreneurs have done in an effort to help others, to create a greater good, and to make this planet a better place for all people. Money is not a bad thing, unless it becomes idolized. Money is nothing more than a tool or a resource to help others in need. I challenge you to become an Affluent Entrepreneur, and then I further challenge you to give your money and time away to help others also create a greater good on our planet.

Finally, I hope you will contact me, share your story of success, and share which principles best served you in your quest to become an Affluent Entrepreneur. My e-mail address is Patrick@PatrickSnow.com. I hope one day to meet you in person as I travel the oceans of the world on my yacht.

I wish you well on your journey. Congratulations on your past successes and all of those soon to come. I know that when you apply these principles to your life, you will realize, experience, create, and enjoy your destiny, all while evolving into the affluent entrepreneur you truly are!

May God bless you!

Your friend,

Patrick Snow

THE 20 CHARACTER TRAITS OF AFFLUENT ENTREPRENEURS

For years, people have been telling me that I am different, more driven, and more determined. It did not take me long to come to agree with them. However, I never really understood why that was the case. As a result of studying the Affluent Entrepreneurs profiled in this book, I have discovered why. Here are the traits that I consider define me as being different and which I amazingly found to match or be similar to those of the Affluent Entrepreneurs profiled in this book. Since you have gotten this far in my book, I suspect you and I are more alike than you think. I ask you now to look inwardly at your own character traits and see whether the traits below that describe Affluent Entrepreneurs also describe you:

1. Always keep their faith and families as a top priority.

2. Learned how to earn money for themselves in their early teens.

3. See their exact visions clearly and never stray from those visions or their beliefs.

4. Quick to identify and take action on a multitude of opportunities.

5. Will begin a project even when the means to achieve the goal is not known, realizing it can be course-corrected as progress is made.

6. Self-confidence that is often mistaken for too big an ego.

7. Driven to accomplish audacious goals and make a difference in the world.

8. Willing to work tirelessly and do whatever it takes to get the job done.

9. Ignore ridicule from others for having an optimistic and dreaming mind-set.

10. Almost always use angel investors to fund enterprises.

11. Interested in mentoring youth of today to become leaders of tomorrow.

12. Independent and do not like or recognize other people's authority over them.

13. Very successful leaders who are not concerned about who or how many are following them.

14. Rule breakers willing to do what is right in order to achieve a greater good.

15. Always taking calculated risks to grow their businesses and serve customers.

16. Fans of underdogs and believers that nothing is impossible in life or business.

17. Fearless in regard to whatever are their missions.

18. Could care less what other people think of them.

19. Extremely passionate and misunderstood by virtually everyone.

20. With hearts as big as goldmines, they reach out to help others in need.

Ask yourself how many of these character traits you possess. If 12 or more, then there is no doubt that you will become an Affluent Entrepreneur and leave a legacy in this world for others to benefit from for hundreds of years to come. If fewer than 12, then you may want to keep your day job, play it safe, and live a life of mediocrity, never really making a difference in this world.

THE AFFLUENT ENTREPRENEUR'S CREED

From this day forward, I will make the world a better place. My work, my commitment, and the results of my business ventures will enrich my community, my country, and my planet. I commit to the following:

1. In everything I do, I will never forget that faith and family are my first priority. I will always fight like hell to preserve and honor both.

2. I will seek to generate revenue, focusing on prospecting and leaving the tasks I dislike or am not good at to others.

3. I will create a clear vision of what I want and then live that vision as if it has already happened until it becomes my reality.

4. When opportunity knocks, I will be the first to open the door so I may welcome success.

5. I will begin a project even when I don't know how the goal will be achieved, realizing that I will course-correct as progress is made.

6. I will exude confidence in what I do, and if others think my ego is too big, I will know I am succeeding.

7. "It can't be done" is not in my vocabulary. I will prove it can be done and change what people believe is possible.

8. No matter how formidable the task at hand, I will stay at it until the job is done, knowing the reward will be many times the efforts I make.

9. I will follow my dreams, no matter how unrealistic they seem. I will trust in myself and confidently know that I will see it when I believe it.

10. I will not only give others fish, but I will teach them to fish for themselves.

11. I will mentor the next generation to become the entrepreneurial leaders of tomorrow.

12. I will work for myself, rather than others. I will be my own boss and let no one else have authority over me.

13. Rather than being a follower, I will be a trailblazer, creating the path for others to follow.

14. I will not limit myself to someone else's rules or beliefs but do what is necessary to achieve a greater good.

15. I will take the necessary calculated risks for the good of myself, my business, my employees or business associates, and my customers.

16. I will fight for the underdogs and be a living example that nothing is impossible in life or business.

17. Whatever I must do, no matter how frightening it is, I will step forward confidently, remembering there is nothing to fear but fear itself, and I will find a way to succeed.

18. I will never let someone else's opinion of me determine my reality.

19. Even if no one else agrees or understands me, I will stay true to my dreams and follow my passions.

20. I commit the rest of my life to achieving prosperity so that I can give of both my time and my money to those in need. By doing so, I will leave behind my legacy and know I have truly succeeded at being an Affluent Entrepreneur.

About the Author

Patrick Snow is an international best-selling author, professional keynote speaker, publishing coach, and Internet entrepreneur. He firmly believes we can all achieve our individual and organizational destinies when we *"Dream, Plan, Execute, and Soar."* Patrick Snow has electrified and inspired more than 1,500 audiences worldwide over the last 20 years to create their own destinies and get exactly what they want out of life and work. Today, he is known as "The Dean of Destiny" by high achievers worldwide.

After being laid off following 9/11 and then again in 2002 from high-tech sales, Patrick retired from corporate America on his own terms at 36 years of age to live the entrepreneurial life he loves. Today, at age 42, he guides and inspires others to turn their career distress into personal success by applying leadership principles, embracing change, balancing family and work, and achieving one's visions!

Patrick discovered his gift for speaking in the fall of 1986 at age 17. As the captain of his high school varsity football team, he delivered the pregame speeches that inspired his team members to perform at their highest levels. At that moment, he knew that inspiring others to achieve extraordinary results both at work and at home was his passion in life.

Patrick's "destiny" message has been profiled in the *New York Times*, *Denver Post*, and the *Chicago Sun-Times*. His best-selling book, *Creating Your Own Destiny: How to Get Exactly What You Want Out of Life and Work*, and his personal transition were also featured as a cover story in *USA TODAY*. Patrick's first book has been translated into numerous foreign languages and has sold more than 150,000 copies across six continents since 2001.

John Wiley & Sons, Inc., published the revised and updated version of *Creating Your Own Destiny*. Patrick's second book,

The Affluent Entrepreneur: 20 Proven Principles for Achieving Prosperity, was published by Wiley in late 2010. Patrick is also a contributing author to numerous other books including the new *Chicken Soup for the Soul: Life Lessons for Mastering the Law of Attraction*.

To date, Patrick has coached more than 250 clients in achieving their goals of writing, publishing, and marketing their books. He's coached thousands of others to build their businesses and organizations on limited budgets using his "Sales Success Formula" and "Destiny Secret." His warm-hearted style and passion for helping others achieve stunning results in their lives, careers, and businesses fuels lasting friendships and invites expressions of gratitude from those who follow his time-tested, from-the-trenches, proven system.

Originally from Michigan, Patrick graduated from the University of Montana in 1991. He and his two sons, Samuel and Jacob, reside together on Bainbridge Island, Washington.

ABOUT THE SNOW GROUP

After 10 years of speaking, writing, and coaching part time, Patrick Snow successfully launched The Snow Group as a sole proprietorship at the turn of the millennium on January 1, 2000. Since then, his message has been well received globally, and his book *Creating Your Own Destiny* has been translated into numerous languages throughout the world. Patrick Snow has spoken worldwide and has clients on six different continents.

The mission of The Snow Group is to help people worldwide overcome their fears, turn their career distress into personal success, and help others attain more time, more money, more freedom, more health, more love, and more happiness in life. As a business-ownership advocate, Patrick Snow is dedicated to helping others apply his free enterprise philosophy to their lives and achieve wealth and prosperity through capitalism. The Snow Group concentrates its energy in four areas:

1. Author: His books are available at volume discounts and in numerous foreign languages.

2. Speaker: Patrick will tailor his speech to address your needs. www.PatrickSnow.com

3. Coach: Patrick helps entrepreneurs become best-selling authors. www.BestSellerBookCoaching.com

4. Internet Entrepreneur: www.NumisNetwork.com/Patrick Snow

For a 30-minute, complimentary consultation or price quote, please visit www.PatrickSnow.com.

BEST-SELLER BOOK COACHING

Patrick Snow has been successfully coaching entrepreneurs on how to get published, become bestselling authors, highly paid speakers, and sought after coaches since 2002. His unique publishing coaching, book promotion coaching, and speaker coaching road map simplifies the process of creating a book and taking it to market. Patrick's system has taken more than 15 years to develop and he currently publishes books for about 50 clients each year. This system includes one-on-one coaching, weekly conference calls, and personal mentoring directly from Patrick Snow. He offers his Best-Seller Publishing Institute at different tropical locales several times a year. See www.BestSellerBookCoaching .com for dates and registration information.

Book Publishing: Patrick's unique road map will take your vision and turn it into a published book within 3 to 12 months. Your book will then serve as a lead-generating tool for your platform that will help grow your speaking, coaching, and consulting practice.

Book Promotion: Patrick's book marketing program will assist you in creating a best seller. His system will get you into major newspapers, TV, and radio. He will help you find foreign publishers that will help translate your book into numerous languages.

Speaker Coaching: Patrick's experience as an international keynote professional speaker gives him the knowledge to help you double or even triple your speaker fees. He will share with you his speaking formula that will keep your speaking calendar full.

For a 30-minute, complimentary publishing consultation, contact: www.BestSellerBookCoaching.com.

Book Patrick Snow to Speak at Your Next Event

When it comes to choosing a professional speaker for your next event, you'll find no one more respected or successful—no one who will leave your audiences or colleagues with such a renewed passion for life—than Patrick Snow, one of the most gifted speakers of our generation. Since 1986, Patrick has delivered more than 1,500 customized presentations.

Whether your audience is 10 or 10,000, in North America or abroad, Patrick Snow can deliver a tailor-made message of inspiration for your meeting or conference. Patrick's speaking philosophy is that he fully understands your audience does not want to be "taught" anything. Rather they are interested in hearing stories of inspiration, achievement, and real-life people achieving their destinies.

As a result Patrick Snow's style of speaking is to humor, entertain, and inspire your audience with passion and stories proven to help your audience achieve extraordinary results. If you are looking for a memorable speaker who will leave your audience wanting more, then book Patrick Snow today.

To see a highlight video of Patrick Snow and learn whether he is available for your next meeting, visit his web site below and then contact him to schedule a complimentary prespeech interview:

www.TheAffluentEntrepreneur.com
Patrick@PatrickSnow.com
www.PatrickSnow.com
(206) 780-1787

INDEX